CONTROLLING YOUR CLASS

CONTROLLING YOUR CLASS

A Teacher's Guide to Managing Classroom Behaviour

Bill McPhillimy

JOHN WILEY & SONS

Chichester · New York · Brisbane · Toronto · Singapore

Copyright © 1996 by John Wiley & Sons Ltd,
Baffins Lane, Chichester,
West Sussex PO19 1UD, England

National   01243 779777
International (+44) 1243 779777
e-mail (for orders and customer service enquiries):
cs-books@wiley.co.uk
Visit our Home Page on http://www.wiley.co.uk
             or http://www.wiley.com

Cartoons © 1996 by Ian Stuart

Other Wiley Editorial Offices

John Wiley & Sons, Inc., 605 Third Avenue,
New York, NY 10158–0012, USA

Jacaranda Wiley Ltd, 33 Park Road, Milton,
Queensland 4064, Australia

John Wiley & Sons (Canada) Ltd, 22 Worcester Road,
Rexdale, Ontario M9W 1LI, Canada

John Wiley & Sons (Asia) Pte Ltd, 2 Clementi Loop #02–01,
Jin Xing Distripark, Singapore 0512

Library of Congress Cataloging-in-Publication Data

McPhillimy, Bill.
    Controlling your class : a teacher's guide to managing classroom
behaviour / Bill McPhillimy.
       p.   cm.
    Includes bibliographical references.
    ISBN 0-471-96568-5 (pbk.)
    1. Classroom management.   I. Title.
LB3013.M3877   1996
371.1'024—dc20   96–25546
                                                      CIP

British Library Cataloguing in Publication Data
A catalogue record for this book is available from the British Library

ISBN 0-471-96568-5

Typeset in 11/13pt Palatino by Dorwyn Ltd, Rowlands Castle
Printed and bound in Great Britain by Bookcraft (Bath) Ltd
This book is printed on acid-free paper responsibly manufactured from sustainable
forestation, for which at least two trees are planted for each one used for paper
production.

CONTENTS

About the author   vii

Preface   ix

1   Four fallacies   1

Four frequently offered 'answers' to the problems of
control are examined. These are: (i) that most misbehaviour stems from pupils' psychological problems; (ii) that 'changing the system' in schools or in
society in general will eliminate misbehaviour; (iii)
that 'making the work interesting' is the solution;
and (iv) that it is all a matter of the strength of the
teacher's personality. While these all contain some
truth, they are viewed as being unhelpful and mis-
leading to a teacher struggling with control
problems.

2   Personal qualities   19

The personal qualities—personality characteristics,
attitudes, and demeanour—which help teachers to
cope with control difficulties are examined. How
these qualities can be developed and more clearly
presented to pupils is discussed.

3   Organisational and interpersonal strategies   33

A range of preventative strategies which make misbehaviour less likely to occur is outlined. These include the organisation of work and resources, the
establishment of rules, and ways of making pupils
feel accountable.

4 A behavioural, reflective, relationship (BRR) approach 53
An approach to behaviour and misbehaviour drawn
from behavioural and cognitive psychology is proposed. Ideas from these two standpoints, often seen
as incompatible, are examined; some are rejected but
others are combined into an approach which involves
the reflective use of behavioural techniques such as
reward and punishment within a mutually positive
teacher–pupil relationship.

5 Putting the BRR approach into practice 69
The principles developed in chapter 4 are applied to
produce an account of how a teacher with a new class
or set of classes might set about creating and maintaining good control and relationships.

6 The BRR approach in action 97
Five real-life case-studies are presented, two from
primary school and three from secondary.

7 Perennial problems 123
Some of the difficulties teachers most frequently encounter are examined and 'answered' from a BRR
standpoint.

A last word 143
Some suggested further reading 145
Index 147

ABOUT THE AUTHOR

Bill McPhillimy is a Chartered Psychologist and has been a schoolteacher, school psychologist and lecturer in Educational Studies at Northern College, Aberdeen, involved with under-graduate, postgraduate and in-service courses for primary and secondary teachers. He is now co-editor of *Education in the North* (the Journal of Scottish Education) and an associate lecturer at the college.

PREFACE

This book has two simple linked intentions: first, to help teachers, especially beginning teachers, to achieve better control of their classes, and, second, to help them to feel less anxious and guilty about the difficulties they experience in trying to do so. It is not an academic treatise in which there is an attempt to justify all the points made and advice given by reference to research or other evidence. There is, in fact, evidence which could be led at length to justify much of what is offered, but what I have tried to do instead is to digest a great deal of information into a short, readable set of ideas and guidelines which a busy student or teacher might readily relate to her own experience and try to put into practice. The inclusion of multiple references in a text like this would interrupt the flow and tend to distract the reader from the main task in hand, that is to relate what she is reading to her own views, feelings and experiences.

A fair amount of what I say can also be found in one or other of the many volumes on this topic. What I have attempted to do is: (i) to select what I think are the most useful ideas from this literature; (ii) to consider and develop these in the light of my own experience of teaching and of what I have learned at second-hand from others' experience; and (iii) to synthesise the results of this into something clear, coherent and practicable enough to be called an 'approach'.

This approach I have called a *behavioural, reflective, relationship approach*. It is behavioural in that it focuses on what pupils do and say and the teacher's need sometimes to change this; it is reflective in that it involves deciding upon strategies to bring about these changes in the light of an understanding of pupils' motivations and their perceptions of themselves, their situations and their teachers; and it is a relationship approach in that it acknowledges that many of the best strategies for change require a mutual positive relationship between pupil and teacher.

The advice given may seem to some readers to be rather directive. However, this is only because I want to make it quite clear what I think, not because I want to tell you what to think. I know that in areas like this one there is always an 'on the other hand', and that every teacher eventually forms her own unique approach to class control. I hope the ideas offered here will contribute significantly to yours, but the questions at the end of each chapter will give you an opportunity to disagree with them, ideally in the course of a discussion with other teachers or students. Such discussion and study might be aided by the lists of main points ('useful principles' for chapters 6 and 7, which consist of exemplification) also placed at the ends of the chapters.

As I have said above, there are no references given in what follows. However, I have suggested some further reading at the end of the book, and I wish to emphasise my debt to the writers of the books and articles I have read over the years. If you want to follow up any of the ideas discussed you will find no shortage of material on the library shelves.

I should also like to thank my former colleagues Ralph Dutch, Iain Maclean and Jim Towers for helping me to clarify my ideas on this complex topic, Pat Sim for word-processing most of the text, Ian Stuart for his cartoons, the many teachers and students from whose insights I have benefited, and, especially, my wife Dorothy, whose experience as a teacher and headteacher with class duties over more than twenty years has been one of my main sources.

Throughout I have referred to the teacher as 'she' and the pupil as 'he'. This makes for clarity and ease of expression and incidentally reflects the facts that most of the teachers and student

teachers I have known have been female and most of the misbehaving pupils have been boys. I am well aware, however, that
both males and females can fill either role. As I deal with both
primary and secondary schools, I have normally used the term
'pupil' as a halfway house between the rather young-sounding
'child' and the more fashionable but rather old-sounding
'student'.

1

FOUR FALLACIES

The subject of class control or 'discipline' is one of the most sensitive topics to discuss with teachers or student teachers. Why should this be so? I think the main reason for this is that there is no aspect of teaching in which a teacher feels she is more 'on the line' as a person than in her ability to 'control the class', that is, (i) to be able to create an orderly classroom in which the children get on with their work and behave politely and reasonably, and (ii) to be able to deal successfully with disruption or defiance if these arise. However good or bad other aspects of your teaching might be, if you can achieve these things, you tend to feel good about yourself and be highly regarded by colleagues and pupils. Other difficulties, we tend to feel, can be readily dealt with, if we so choose, by devoting time and energy to them, but if you 'can't control your class', you are quite likely to feel guilty about it and inadequate as a person. Even when a teacher's control problems aren't extreme, such feelings are often experienced.

Different teachers deal with these feelings in different ways. One common way is by pretending to others that the control problems don't exist—by keeping the classroom door closed (both literally and metaphorically) and by assuring colleagues that everything is fine, while knowing that it isn't and becoming more and more anxious and distressed. Another way of surviving is to pretend not only to others but to yourself that the misbehaviour is not misbehaviour at all: 'That's just my way of working—I like to give them freedom to express themselves.' Teachers who adopt this strategy have become detached from two important realities—that the pupils are behaving badly and that something should be done about it.

'That's just my way of working—I like to give them freedom to express themselves.'

The very personal sense of failure involved in having problems of control makes it difficult for teachers to seek and to be given help. It is relatively easy to tell a senior colleague that you feel you are not coping adequately with, say, developing pupils' discussion skills and would value some advice, but it is much harder to say the same sort of thing about your class control. The former seems to be simply a matter of knowledge or techniques that have to be acquired or developed, while the second feels as though it is largely a matter of personal adequacy.

The first and perhaps most important step in dealing with the control problems you experience is therefore to face up to them, and to put aside the feelings of guilt and inadequacy that make it difficult to do so. This is more easily said than done, of course, but there are two things which will definitely help. First, tell yourself that you are not alone. Consider this statement: '99% of teachers admit they have had control problems at one time or another; 1% are liars or very forgetful.' This is not, of course, a research finding, merely my opinion based on experience, but I believe most teachers (perhaps about 99% of them) would agree with it. Even those teachers with apparently magical control will normally readily admit that things were not always so easy for them; that through experience they have acquired attitudes and techniques that allow them to create the classroom atmosphere that so impresses others.

Second, tell yourself that it is unprofessional and irresponsible to conceal or deny control problems. Such difficulties will inevitably result in harm to pupils' learning and development (and perhaps even in physical harm). By acknowledging them to yourself and others, which is the first step in getting something done to deal with them, you are being a morally better person (and certainly a more professional teacher) than if you deny or conceal them. Any senior colleague worthy of his or her salt will regard you more favourably if you acknowledge such problems and ask for advice or support than if you pretend to yourself or others that they do not exist.

There is, however, a great deal that a teacher can do to establish good control, short of turning to senior colleagues for help, although, as just suggested, this is a step that should not be avoided when necessary. In this book, I intend to explore possible answers to the problems of control, including both ones I consider useful, and, to begin with, ones I consider unhelpful and even damaging to the interests of both pupils and teachers. I believe that much of the anxiety and unhappiness that teachers with control problems experience, and, indeed, some of the problems themselves, stem from frequently-stated, plausible, but essentially wrong-headed views about control held by various sorts of 'experts' and, indeed, practitioners themselves. These views I consider to be fallacies; time and again they crop up in reading and discussion, and I feel that they have to be dealt with and set aside before consideration of constructive action can begin. They are: (i) a psychological fallacy; (ii) a so-ciological fallacy; (iii) the 'interest' fallacy; and (iv) the staffroom cynic's fallacy. Each of them requires detailed consideration, which now follows.

(i) A psychological fallacy

This is the view that pupils' misbehaviour in class stems mainly from psychological disturbance related to pupils' personal prob-lems, such as difficulties with relationships at home. Mis-behaviour is seen as a symptom of this disturbance and a sign that a pupil needs help with his difficulties, rather than as some-thing which is primarily important in that it is having a disrup-tive effect on the learning of the pupil concerned and the rest of the class. How accurate is this 'disturbance' view and how help-ful is it to the teacher? To start with, it has to be agreed that some misbehaviour in class is probably of this nature. Having said this, three questions arise. First, how frequently is misbehaviour due to such causes? Second, what should be done about this kind of behaviour? Third, what are the likely results of treating all or most misbehaviour as having such causes?

The answer to the first question cannot be given objectively, since no-one has carried out the research (if such research were possible) which would be required to provide a definitive an-swer. Instead, we have to turn to experience and common sense. To begin, ask yourself these questions. When you were a school pupil and misbehaved, how often was this due, as far as you know, to your personal problems and consequent psychological disturbance? When you saw other pupils misbehave, how often did you think then, and do you think now, that this was due to psychological disturbance? I have asked teachers and students these questions many times, and their consensus answer (and mine) to both has been, 'Hardly ever'.

Next, consider this scene. Class 7 are engaged in creative craft work, under the guidance of the new student. They are enjoying themselves, and getting excited. Some children are smearing others' clothes with paint, some are propelling dollops of papier mâché at the ceiling with rulers. A fist fight has broken out between two girls. The student is helping a tearful boy to look for his missing glasses and lunch box. The noise increases to a tumult, finally penetrating as far as the staffroom, where the class teacher, a calm, experienced and forceful woman, sighs, gets up from her marking, walks along the corridor and opens the classroom door with a noisy flourish. What happens next? As you know (were you once in that class?), the uproar ceases almost instantly, pupils trying in mid-movement to convert their actions into legitimate ones, fist-fighters freezing as if on video when they become aware of the hush, the student looking up, blinking in surprise. The lesson from this little drama is, of course, that all this misbehaviour, far from being the result of psychological disturbance, is, in fact, a product of the situation (created by teacher and student) in which pupils have found themselves, together, of course, with what should never be forgotten, the playfulness and mischievousness of the young of the human species.

If further proof of this is needed, try 'shadowing' a secondary school class for a day as it goes round the school from one subject to another. Students who do this are frequently amazed at how the behaviour of the same pupils can differ from teacher to teacher. Is it likely that they are psychologically stable in the classroom of Miss Wise of the Maths department, but that most of them become almost instantly disturbed once they come under the influence of Mr Strange, the English teacher? Clearly, no. So the answer to the first of the three questions asked above, that is how much misbehaviour can be attributed to psychological disturbance, is that probably relatively little everyday misbehaviour is of this kind, and that most of it is caused by pupils' mischievousness and playfulness and the situations, events and relationships within their classrooms. The causes of such misbehaviour are often less serious than its disruptive effects.

This brings us to the second question. What should teachers do about 'disturbed' misbehaviour, relatively infrequent though it might be? Since it is often very difficult to decide when misbehaviour is due to disturbance rather than to high spirits, boredom, etc., the rule should be to treat it as 'normal' misbehaviour until it becomes clear that it is not. Unless the misbehaviour is very extreme or bizarre, this may take some time. If this seems somewhat hard on a possibly disturbed pupil, remember that what you are doing is giving him the benefit of the doubt, that is, doing the charitable thing of treating him as normal until you are sure this is not the case. When normal treatment is ineffective, and you suspect that the misbehaviour is probably due to disturbance, then you should seek expert help, through senior staff, and continue to try to improve the pupil's behaviour in the light of the advice given, in ways that are compatible with keeping generally good overall class control.

The third question posed above concerns the effects of regarding all or most misbehaviour as stemming from psychological disturbance. If a teacher takes this view, then certain consequences are likely to follow. First, the misbehaviour is seen as relatively unimportant in itself, and is therefore likely to be allowed to continue while attempts are made to deal with the real or supposed underlying disturbance. This, especially if more than one or two pupils are involved, is likely to have devastatingly disruptive effects on the work of the class. A teacher cannot forget that her prime concern is to foster pupils' learning. If pupils' misbehaviour is tolerated in the real or supposed interest of their mental health to an extent where the education of others (and themselves) is seriously disrupted, then the teacher is not doing her main job. This does not mean that a teacher should not be understanding and sympathetic with regard to pupils' personal problems, or concerned about their mental health, simply that what she does about these things must be compatible with the aim of maintaining an orderly classroom in which it is possible for all pupils to work and learn. If a teacher believes that most or all misbehaviour is due to psychological disturbance or personal problems and gives her prime concern to helping to deal with these, then it becomes virtually impossible to teach in any conventional sense—instead of teaching a class, she would be engaged in some kind of group therapy, run for the supposed benefit of the misbehavers, at the expense of the other pupils. This is not what teachers are trained for, paid for or expected to do by pupils and parents. Teachers are not therapists whose duty is to help clients to become better adjusted—such a role can be, at most, only a secondary one for them. In short, therefore, the effect of regarding misbehaviour as solely or mainly resulting from psychological disturbance or pupils' personal problems would be to turn the classroom from a place of learning into something with a focus quite different from that of teaching, a psychological clinic, rather than a classroom.

The above argument can be summed up as follows:

(1) Psychological disturbance, resulting from personal problems, is not the main cause of misbehaviour in classrooms.

(2) When it is suspected that a pupil's misbehaviour is due to such causes, give him the benefit of the doubt by regarding the misbehaviour as ordinary everyday misbehaviour and responding to it as such.

(3) If this is not effective, seek expert help (via senior staff) for the pupil.

(4) In collaboration with such a helper, seek and apply techniques which will help this pupil to behave in the classroom in ways which do not disrupt his own or others' learning.

(5) If therapy or counselling is undertaken by the helper, co-operate in any way that might be requested.

It should not be assumed, incidentally, that this businesslike approach, which may well involve setting and enforcing limits (in (2) or (4) above) for a disturbed pupil will not be to his liking. Such pupils often see such limits and treatment as evidence that the teacher cares about how they behave, and may see a permissive approach as indicative of indifference as to how they behave and what harm they do themselves.

(ii) A sociological fallacy

This fallacy can be summed up by the slogan: 'Change the system!' This injunction, stemming from a left-wing sociological standpoint, has been directed at both the small-scale systems, within the school and classroom, and the larger-scale system of our society itself. The kind of person who would argue these cases might have been annoyed by certain assumptions I have made earlier. For instance, I have not hesitated to label pupils' activities disruptive to the teacher-set work of the class as 'misbehaviour'. This person would question this, pointing out logically that such behaviour is only misbehaviour because it breaks certain teacher-set or school-set rules.

A connected assumption I have made is that teachers and schools are entitled to set such rules and to try to change the behaviour of those who break them. Such authority can be questioned, of course. Why should school pupils, who are frequently in school reluctantly and sometimes directly against their will, conform to such rules? Misbehaviour could disappear overnight with appropriate changes to school rules, that is, if the system within the school were changed. It could be made acceptable to absent oneself from school, to do only the work one wanted to, to engage in chat when the teacher wanted silence, and so on. If all these things were acceptable, teacher 'control' would no longer be needed and there would therefore be no control problems. The fallacy here, of course, is that it is pointless to talk of eliminating control problems in this way, when to do so would be simply to legitimise behaviour that most pupils, parents, teachers and the public in general do not wish to legitimise. Parents would not feel their children would learn in a school with such a system, and, indeed, might fear for their children's safety.

As previously stated, 'changing the system' is also suggested on a wider scale than just outlined. That is, it is argued that the structure of our society is such, through inequalities of various kinds, that large-scale social changes to lessen these inequalities are necessary before we can fairly expect pupils to behave well in school. Taking such a viewpoint, the mis-behaviour of pupils in schools is seen as symptomatic of, and even a conscious protest against, the social disadvantages of the misbehaving pupils. If this is so, the argument runs, there is little point trying to counter misbehaviour in schools; indeed it can be seen as a good thing, a stimulus to change. This kind of argument was commonplace in the 1960s and 70s and con-tinues to be made from time to time. However, it is as fallacious now as it was then, on at least three counts. First, it assumes, like the psychological fallacy above, that most misbehaviour in school has serious causes, in this case, injustice in society, when, in fact, most people from their own experience would probably agree that misbehaviour is largely playful, mis-chievous behaviour, determined by the situations pupils find themselves in. For every 'protest against society' that takes place in classrooms, I would bet that there are at least a thou-sand instances of 'larking about'. Second, misbehaviour in school is clearly not restricted to the disadvantaged, as anyone who (like me) has been a pupil and teacher at advantaged and disadvantaged schools will surely agree. The third and most important count is that accepting this point of view would lead a teacher to stand back and accept disruptive behaviour, thus harming the pupils in her care for the supposed benefit of hypothetical future pupils. How can this possibly be justified? If people want to 'change the system' in such radical ways, then they should surely attempt to do this by political means, not by allowing pupils to disrupt their own and others' school learning.

So changing the system is not the answer. What about the other possibilities?

(iii) The interest fallacy

I have heard this fallacy from many sources, including some college lecturers and headteachers. It is the widely held view that the answer to control problems is to 'make the work interesting'. Teachers whose pupils misbehave are told that this happens because the pupils do not find their work interesting and are therefore easily distracted into misbehaviour. The misbehaviour is thus seen again as a symptom rather than something to be directly addressed. The teacher with control problems is asked to work harder on preparation, presentation and matching of work to pupils' needs and desires. If these things are well-enough done, according to this view, pupils will become fully engaged with their work and will have no wish or need to misbehave. This 'answer' has obvious attractions for an irresponsible or misguided college tutor, headteacher or head of department (and some do exist) who is asked for help with problems of control. For one thing, it throws the blame and the responsibility for solving the problem squarely on the student or teacher, and absolves the senior person from having to produce guidance on behaviour management. For another, it is an answer that cannot be proven wrong. If pupils still misbehave after the teacher has tried to make the work more interesting, then 'obviously' she has failed to achieve this, and is still at fault. She must therefore try harder.

This particular view, that making the work interesting is the answer to misbehaviour, is, I think, a particularly counter-productive one. Not only is it wrong, which I intend to show soon, but it misdirects teachers in their efforts to cope, leading to them spending more and more time fruitlessly on preparation, becoming more and more exhausted while their feelings of guilt and failure increase. In what ways is it wrong? Before answering this question, it must be acknowledged that, as with many fallacies, there is something of substance in this view. Obviously, if a pupil is fully engaged by a task he has been set, he is less likely to misbehave. For this reason among others, therefore, teachers should certainly always try to make their pupils' work interesting. However, to suggest that this is the complete or even main answer, is, I believe, quite wrong, for at least four good reasons, which I now intend to explore at some length, as I believe this fallacy is one that must be exposed at all costs.

First, to argue that it is a teacher's job to prepare and present work so well that it is interesting to all of her pupils all of the time is ludicrously unfair and impracticable. The superteacher who is capable of this is a very rare creature indeed. Second, there are things which pupils have to learn (often because they are required for future learning), but which are not, in themselves, particularly interesting or capable of being made interesting. For example, all pupils need to learn reference skills in order to be able to use dictionaries and encyclopaedias. To learn these skills, intensive practice in 'finding the entry', etc., is necessary. It is not sufficient for pupils just to look things up now and again when the occasion arises, as the time gaps between such tasks militate against the internalisation of the procedures necessary for quick and accurate access. Yet such repetitive practice of reference skills is not particularly interesting to most pupils. This does not mean it should not be done, but it does mean that control techniques other than 'having interesting work' are necessary for conscientious teachers. Third, a teacher will often produce work which pupils find interesting, but from which they are distracted by something more interesting. How interesting would work have to be made for pupils to continue with it while ignoring another pupil having a spectacular nosebleed, a large digger starting to rip up the playground outside the classroom window, or a chum being outrageously cheeky to the teacher? It is impossible for work to be made sufficiently interesting to defeat all the possible distractions of classroom life.

If these reasons are not sufficient to refute 'making the work interesting' as the answer to misbehaviour, there is a fourth, even more powerful, one to consider. If you offered a book to a friend to read, saying that you thought he would find it interesting, but your friend, after glancing at the cover, said that it was boring, what would you do? I think you would probably tell your friend that he could not really make such a judgment until he had looked more seriously at the book, reading a substantial part of it. In the same way, it is surely the case that a school pupil cannot, fairly, decide that a lesson or set task is uninteresting to

'It is impossible for work to be made sufficiently interesting to defeat
all the possible distractions of classroom life.'

him without taking it seriously, that is, paying close attention to
the lesson or making a serious attempt at the task. In other
words, good behaviour is quite often likely to be necessary *before*
pupils can find work interesting, for interest is not something
that resides in the lesson or learning activity, but within the
pupil, and is the product of significant interaction between pupil
and lesson. If this interaction does not take place, due to misbehaviour, then, logically, it is impossible for the work to be
found interesting. Thus good control, leading to good behaviour, is likely to be a necessary prerequisite for interest,
rather than result from it.

In my experience, this 'answer' to the problem of control has
been an extremely counter-productive one, leading to an enor-
mous amount of anxiety, unhappiness and wasted effort for
teachers. Making the work interesting is always desirable and
will help with control, but it is not the sole or main answer to the
problems, and to advise a teacher experiencing control problems

to spend more and more of her time and energy on such a wild-goose chase is not only futile, but will often make matters worse, as it will lead to the teacher becoming more and more tired, anxious and unhappy and thus less able to deal with misbehaving pupils.

If any reader is still unconvinced of the wrong-headedness of this view, then perhaps the following true story will do the trick. Many years ago, as a newly qualified secondary teacher of English, I was given, in the traditional way, the most difficult class in the school, the bottom stream of the third year, which was then the last compulsory year of schooling. This class, unlike all the others in the year, contained only boys, on the grounds that these particular boys were deemed unfit to mix with girls. Almost all of the boys disliked school and teachers, many were very badly behaved, and some were downright aggressive. Part of my job, as I saw it, was to try to get them to begin to see some value in books and reading, which might lead them to maintain such an interest after the largely unsuccessful force-feeding of school was over for them. As a means to this end, I held a class discussion about the merits of the books currently being offered for sale through a book-club which circulated a monthly sales pamphlet in the school. I offered to buy and read to them the book they, as a group, would most like to hear. After a fairly chaotic discussion and a surprisingly solemnly-held vote, they settled for a ghosted autobiography of the then young footballer (I said it was a long time ago), George Best.

When the book arrived, they were keen to hear it. However, I am sad to say that despite starting to read it to them with great enthusiasm and high hopes of a crucial breakthrough, I got no further than the third page. Even with the best will in the world to read in a lively way and make lots of eye-contact, it is not possible to read to a class without sometimes looking at the page. Virtually every time I did so, misbehaviour broke out. Wind was broken, both mock and real, books flew through the air, minor assaults were perpetrated on boys in front, and so on. Georgie Best was abandoned, along with my high hopes of a literary breakthrough. Was this because I was wrong to think they would be interested in George Best? This hardly seems likely. They were almost all football-mad, Georgie was already a cult figure, only a few years older than themselves, and they had chosen the book. No; if they had taken my reading of the book seriously, actually listened to it, they would have found it interesting.

I proved this, at least to my own satisfaction, the next year. As a reward for having survived, I was given the corresponding class of boys again. Determined to get my money's worth, I decided to read George Best to them. This time I waited until after Christmas, by which time I had fairly good control. Although this class had not chosen the book, they listened attentively and enjoyed it. We were never in any danger of not reaching the end. The message to me at the time was simple. Make the work interesting, yes, but get them to behave themselves first, so that the interesting work will not be wasted.

So much for the interest fallacy. Now to the last of the set.

(iv) The staffroom cynic's fallacy

I attribute this one to the staffroom cynic—the experienced, un-enthusiastic survivor, sceptical about educational ideas, de-velopments and theories old and new. However, it might also be called the layman's fallacy, because it is frequently expressed by non-teachers. As a view, it is one which is guaranteed to send a chill down the spine of the student or teacher struggling with control problems, and is usually expressed along the lines of: 'It's all a matter of personality.' In other words, if you have a good, strong personality, your pupils will behave well; if you can't get them to behave, it is because you don't have a strong enough personality, and nothing much can be done about it.

As with the other fallacies, there is, of course, something in this one, and most teachers (including me) who have had control problems will have wondered at times whether it is true. The personality, attitudes and general demeanour towards pupils of a teacher certainly are factors which play a part in determining success or failure with regard to control, and this will be dealt with later. At the moment, however, we must consider whether 'It's *all* a matter of personality.' If this were the case, we would have a strange situation. People entering teaching would be capable of division into two groups: those with personalities which would lead to pupils behaving well, and those with personalities which would lead to pupils behaving badly. However, on any given personality dimension, people vary from one extreme to the other, with most in the middle range, rather than falling into two distinct groups. If the personality characteristics which determine good class control could be identified and people's possession of them measured, what would be found would not be two distinct groups—the haves and have-nots—but, if anything, three groups—a small group who possess the characteristics in abundance, a small group who hardly possess them at all, and, in the middle, the bulk of the population.

Just as we cannot restrict teaching to the few superteachers who can make everything interesting to everyone all the time, we cannot restrict it to the few with superpersonalities. The few teachers in the unsuitable personality group will have great difficulty coping, and have perhaps chosen the wrong career, but the great majority in the middle group can, by learning and applying techniques and adopting certain attitudes and ways of behaving, readily improve their ability to control pupils. The personality attributes, attitudes and techniques conducive to good control will be dealt with later. At the moment, what is important is to underline that the staffroom cynic is wrong. It is not all a matter of personality. Most teachers can learn to cope with the problems of control.

The four fallacies have now been dealt with, and, I hope, successfully refuted as embodying, in each of their different ways, 'the answer' to control problems. I think they are all counterproductive. The fact that each has some truth in it is perhaps the most dangerous aspect of them, because it is this element of truth that allows them to flourish and mislead and distress teachers having control problems. Before turning to the positive business of deciding just what can and should be done by a teacher to create good control, these fallacious views have to be set aside. I hope this has now been achieved.

The main points of this chapter

- Failure with class control is often felt as very personal failure and teachers are sensitive about discussing their difficulties, but the first step in dealing with such problems is to admit and face up to them.

- Virtually all teachers, however competent they seem, have had problems with control at some time.

- There are four less-than-helpful views about control which can be shown to be fallacious.

- The view that misbehaviour results from pupils' psychological problems and should primarily be regarded as a symptom of such disturbance is **a psychological fallacy**.

- While some misbehaviour is no doubt of this nature, most is caused by pupils' playfulness and mischievousness and the social situations in school they find themselves in.

- Until a teacher is fairly sure that a pupil is disturbed, his misbehaviour should be treated as 'normal' misbehaviour; if this doesn't work, expert help should be sought.

- The view that misbehaviour is the result of faults in the small-scale social system of the school or the large-scale system of society and should be primarily regarded as a symptom of these faults is **a sociological fallacy**.

- Dealing with misbehaviour by changing the system within the school (e.g. by eliminating rules) would amount simply to legitimising undesired behaviour.

- Changing society to eliminate injustice, etc., even if possible, would not end misbehaviour in schools, as misbehaviour is not restricted to the disadvantaged and most is not social protest.

- **The interest fallacy** is the view that misbehaviour is the result of the teacher's failure to interest pupils and that making pupils' work interesting is the answer to misbehaviour.

- If a pupil is highly interested in the work he is doing he is certainly much less likely to misbehave.

- However, this is not 'the answer' to misbehaviour for four good reasons: (i) no teacher can prepare and present work so well that it will interest all of her pupils all of the time; (ii) some things which have to be learned are not inherently particularly interesting; (iii) pupils can be distracted from interesting work by something more interesting; (iv) serious attention to work will often be necessary *before* it can be found interesting.

- **The staffroom cynic's fallacy** is the view that a teacher's control depends simply on the strength of her personality.

- A small proportion of teachers do have personal qualities extremely well suited to teaching (and obtaining good control) and a small number are extremely unsuited in this respect.

- Most, however, can learn and apply techniques which will enable them to cope with control problems.

Discussion questions

1. How open with other people have *you* been about the control difficulties you have experienced? How honest have you been to yourself about them? How open and honest have the teachers you have worked with been about the control difficulties they have experienced, in your view? Do teachers in general cover up these problems?

2. In your experience, how much misbehaviour in class is the result of each of the following?
   (i)   Psychological disturbance
   (ii) 'The system' inside and outside the school
   (iii) Pupils' work not being interesting enough
   (iv) Teachers' weaknesses of personality.

   What other causes would you suggest for the misbehaviour you have encountered?

$\boxed{2}$

PERSONAL
QUALITIES

In the previous chapter, I dealt with what I consider to be several fallacious answers to the problem of control. It is now time to try to begin to produce the right answers. When students or teachers want advice on control, the question they usually ask is, 'What should I do?' While this is a very important question, which will be dealt with at length later, I think it is the second question that should be addressed, rather than the first. The first question, in my opinion, that should be asked is, 'What should I be?'; in other words, 'What sort of person is most likely to have good control?' My reason for saying this is that, whatever control strategies or techniques are used, the success or failure of these will depend not just on their intrinsic potential effectiveness, but on whether the teacher is able to use them in appropriate ways. This, in turn, will depend on the kind of person the teacher is, in particular on the attitudes and general ways of behaving she has towards her pupils. In other words, techniques and strategies are never enough by themselves. How pupils perceive the teacher, that is what kind of person she seems to be to them, and what they think she thinks about them, are also crucially important.

Saying this is not tantamount to agreeing with the last of the four fallacies in the last chapter. My view is not that 'It's all a matter of personality', rather that personality, attitudes and demeanour, as well as techniques, are determinants of control, and have to be thought about, and worked on, by teachers who want to improve this aspect of their teaching. For good control is not just a matter of obedience to the teacher's will. What most teachers, most parents and probably most pupils want is for the teacher to be firmly in charge of a class of hardworking, happy pupils, with a relationship of mutual liking and respect between teacher and pupils. Control techniques can certainly help to achieve this, but the personal qualities and attitudes of the teacher are also important.

So, before turning to what teachers should do to achieve good control, the question of what sort of person the teacher should try to be needs to be addressed. In what follows, I am not going to try to discriminate finely between aspects of personality, which are relatively stable, but may be developed or presented more clearly to pupils, and attitudes and demeanour, which are more open to change. What I am going to do is to list and discuss a number of personal qualities which make it more likely, in my view, that a teacher will be able to achieve good control, saying for each why I think this to be the case, and how each quality can be developed and/or better presented to pupils. This list is not meant to be prescriptive, but to suggest only that the more you are able to be like this, the less likely you are to have control difficulties and the more likely you are to be able to overcome them. To a certain extent the qualities overlap (as will be seen) and one very important quality, that is having a sense of humour, is dealt with under several headings rather than being given one of its own. Before going on to deal with the qualities one by one, here is the full list:

(1) Liking pupils and enjoying their company
(2) Believing in the value of learning
(3) Being determined to succeed
(4) Being calm and relaxed
(5) Being a little detached
(6) Being confident
(7) Being thoughtful and analytical
(8) Being open and honest
(9) Thinking positively about yourself.

'. . . the more you are able to be like this, the less likely you are to have control difficulties . . .'

(1) Liking pupils and enjoying their company

This does not mean, of course, that you must like all of your pupils all of the time, but that basically you should have positive feelings towards young people of the age you teach, find them interesting and enjoy spending time with them. You should also be willing to look for and appreciate positive qualities in those you find least likeable. Without such feelings you really shouldn't be a teacher, for you will get little pleasure from your work. From the pupils' point of view, a great deal of what is gained from school, especially at the younger stages, comes not from acquiring skills and knowledge, important as these are, but from good relationships with teachers and the incidental learning of attitudes, interests and moral standards that stems from such relationships. A teacher who doesn't really like children will be unable or unwilling to form such relationships. From the control point of view, it is fairly obvious that a teacher depends a good deal on pupils respecting her and wanting to please her. If she doesn't like them, they will become aware of this and their desire to please will be greatly lessened.

Is liking pupils something that can be acquired? No doubt, with time and appropriate experiences, a person can change in this respect, but the hurly-burly of the first few years of teaching is unlikely to provide such a growth opportunity. Most people who come into teaching, especially at the primary stages, have had enough experience with children to know that they do basically like their company. However, not all are able to show these feelings and to enjoy being with their pupils in their early days in the classroom.

What can be done about this? With time, of course, you will feel more relaxed and less under threat from pupils and begin to show your positive feelings, but one good way to begin to demonstrate and develop mutual liking is by cultivating shared interests with pupils. If, for example, your pupils are interested in certain kinds of music or sport, and if you like your pupils and are interested in them, it is beneficial (and quite natural) to take an interest in these things as well. This is not fake or patronising—it is exactly what people do when they make a new friend. Taking part in extra-curricular activities with pupils is an obvious extension of this beyond the classroom, but of course only some of your pupils (who tend to be the better-behaved) will take part in such activities.

School events and policies are obvious shared interests of teachers and pupils. While, of course, your views may well differ from theirs, honest and open discussion of such matters as homework or uniform, where you take pupils' views seriously and are open to persuasion yourself, help to create a positive mutual relationship. Another means to this end is to make sure that some class time is devoted to activities where pleasant social interaction of an orderly kind, rather than serious work, is the main objective. This is perhaps easier with younger children, with whom games can readily be played. An element of play can often be brought into work—a test, for example, can become a quiz, while still giving information about pupils' learning.

In general, you should look for ways of bringing some light-heartedness into the life of the classroom. Having a sense of humour which allows you to see the funny side of things and make jokes (though if you genuinely like your pupils you will never do so in a hurtful way) is a great asset. If you like your pupils, you should normally be happy in their company and not afraid to show it. The teacher who generally appears cheerful, even when things are difficult, will get across the message that she enjoys the company of the class. If pupils believe that a teacher likes them, it is quite difficult for them not to return at least some of that feeling. To conclude, it is important to note that liking your pupils does not imply that you should be indulgent with them when they misbehave. What it does mean is that you should be sad rather than angry—'disappointed' is a good word to use and way to feel—and your attempts to control misbehaviour should, genuinely, be intended to help pupils to behave better, rather than to effect retribution upon them for having behaved badly.

(2) Believing in the value of learning

Pupils are only human, and do not always see how worthwhile it is to work hard and behave well in school. Sometimes this is because they are young, playful and mischievous. Sometimes, sadly, it is because they feel they are unlikely to achieve very much, no matter how hard they try. Yet the main point of getting them to behave well in class is to create conditions under which they are most likely to learn. Without a strong belief, indeed faith, that what they have to teach is good for pupils to learn, teachers often find it difficult to persist in their efforts to achieve control. Although most teachers begin with such a faith, many lose it later. What you must try to hold on to is that it is very much better for your pupils to know and understand the world, and to acquire some of the skills required to cope with it, than the alternative, which is to be ignorant and lacking in skills. Knowledge, understanding and skills make people better, livelier, more interesting and more able to make life better for themselves and others.

At a lower level, but still a valid point, remember that success at school, in terms of good levels of attainment, and, later, certificates, will usually lead to better opportunities in life. If you can believe these things, you will find it easier to believe, genuinely, that it is good for pupils to behave well, in order to learn and achieve.

(3) Being determined to succeed

To achieve good control, a teacher needs to be determined to achieve the behaviour targets she has set, and to persist doggedly when difficulties are encountered, without becoming counter-productively stubborn, as sometimes targets have to be changed. This need for persistence should never be underestimated. Setbacks in progress towards an orderly classroom are the rule, not the exception. Pupils will persist in previously established patterns of misbehaviour for very long times, and such misbehaviour will re-emerge long after you think it has disappeared. The teacher therefore has to show even greater persistence than the pupils. This kind of determination is naturally possessed more by some teachers than others, and of course, in an extreme degree is a disadvantage, as mentioned above. However, to encourage yourself to persist, try to see your job as long-term, rather than short-term. What matters is not so much what happens now or tomorrow, but what kind of classroom you will have for the rest of the year, and the years after that. Remind yourself that you have a long time with pupils, and it is their long-term learning that matters most. Look for evidence of progress in behaviour (see (7) below), however slight. This should encourage you to persevere, to invest effort and accept difficulties in the early days, in the interest of the long-term benefits for both yourself and your pupils.

(4) Being calm and relaxed

A good deal of pupil misbehaviour is aimed, consciously or unconsciously, at getting the teacher annoyed or upset. The easier some pupils find this to do, the more they are likely to misbehave. Therefore the more calm and relaxed the teacher can be (or appear to be), both generally and when such mis-behaviour takes place, the less likely this kind of misbehaviour becomes. New teachers find it especially difficult to appear re-laxed, largely because they lack confidence (see below), and all of what can be done to increase your confidence will, in turn, help you to be more calm. However, more directly, there are strategies which can help. For example, if you are relaxed, your speech and movement tend to become slower. So, when you are feeling anxious, cultivate a more deliberate way of speaking, pausing before answering, etc., and a slower, smoother way of moving about the room. The old trick of counting to ten (five if this seems too long) before speaking if feeling annoyed can be a real help.

Try not to be, or appear to be, over-anxious for a lesson, demon-stration or set of pupil activities to go well, however hard you have worked to prepare it. Remember teaching is the kind of job where things are always likely to go wrong, but where there will usually be another chance to get them right. Try to be ironic about disasters, rather than disappointed or upset. Looking for the funny side of difficult situations (they normally have one) and sharing a joke about them with pupils can be a great help in keeping things in proportion. Remember how difficult a job (al-most) everyone agrees teaching is, and that perfection, or any-thing near it, is not possible. Being open with colleagues (see below) about your shortcomings is also a help—in general they

will be sympathetic and supportive. Hearing about their difficulties will cheer you up, and will help you to be more relaxed
about your own. Lastly, if you find that you are feeling tense and
anxious most of the time, even out of school, various books on
stress reduction which many people find helpful are available.

(5) Being a little detached

One of the ways to help yourself to cope with misbehaviour is to
be just a little detached in your dealings with pupils in the
classroom. While you like them and care about them, you will
benefit from remembering that your relationship with them is a
professional one—just like a doctor or lawyer, your job is to help
your clients in particular ways. If you get too emotionally involved with them, this can have an adverse effect on the work
you do for them. Teachers who get too close to their pupils are
much more likely to become upset or angry at their misbehaviour, and to see it as directed personally at themselves. As
well as being something which some pupils actually desire (and
which will therefore make them more likely to misbehave), getting angry is also, of course, very wearing emotionally for the
teacher.

Teachers have to remember that they should not be as close to
pupils as parents should be to their children. There are clear
limits as to what teachers can do for, to and with pupils, and to
what aspects of pupils' lives they can become involved in. Parents, as well as being closer, have much more power. They can
become furious with a child, have a row, smack him, produce
tears (perhaps on both sides), send him to his room, and kiss and
make up later when tempers have cooled. Such extremes of
emotion and action are not open to teachers, even if they were
desirable. The teacher is expected to remain calm and businesslike in the interests of the rest of the class—a far larger
number of children than the remainder of any family. This is not
in any way intended to rule out what is obviously desirable for
teachers, that is, that they should be caring and concerned for

their pupils, but simply to try to make clear the nature and limits of that concern, of which the centre should be concern for the learning of each child in the class.

As already mentioned, another justification of the need for detachment is that teachers need to be able not to take misbehaviour personally. Much misbehaviour, although intended to cause the teacher trouble, is directed not so much at the teacher as a person, but as the handiest part of the adult world against which pupils can flex their muscles. With a degree of detachment, it is possible to appreciate this and remain relaxed while taking steps to cope, but without such detachment, it is very difficult not to feel that the misbehaviour is a personal attack or affront and to respond by becoming hurt or angry or both.

(6) Being confident

The teacher who appears quietly confident about her ability to control the class is less likely to be challenged in this respect. Pupils seem able to sense fear or a lack of confidence in a teacher and are much more likely to misbehave and persist in misbehaviour with a teacher who is unsure of herself. Being relaxed, and a little detached, as mentioned above, will help to give an impression of confidence. Being well-prepared, knowing what is supposed to happen in a lesson or activity, having resources ready and allowing enough time for the work in hand, thus avoiding any rush, will all help you to feel and appear more confident. Having clear rules for behaviour in your mind, that is knowing just what you will and will not accept, and knowing exactly what you can and will do in the event of misbehaviour, will also help. With experience, when most of the terrible things that can happen have happened, and you have survived, and when you know that your senior colleagues believe that you are competent, genuine confidence will grow. Until it does, you must do your best to appear confident. If you can manage to keep calm, this will go a long way in achieving this appearance.

(7) Being thoughtful and analytical

A good deal of misbehaviour can be avoided by careful planning and organisation (see chapter 3). Certain types of misbehaviour by certain pupils are likely to occur in certain (often avoidable) situations. Other situations can be created in which misbehaviour is far less likely. To enable yourself to plan and organise like this, you need to be observant, thoughtful and analytical—to note what kinds of events and situations tend to lead to what kinds of behaviour and misbehaviour by individual pupils and by the whole class. To be able to do this, you will need some of the calmness and detachment already mentioned. If you are caught up in a turmoil of emotion, it is very difficult indeed to think clearly about what is going on and extract from it useful information for future use. To help yourself to achieve this, tell yourself that part of your job, as well as teaching your pupils, is to study what is going on in your classroom, in order to make changes that will benefit them and, indeed, your future pupils. Set yourself occasional small observational tasks, for example, to note how many times in 15 minutes a particular child leaves his group, and for what purposes. The more you do this sort of thing, consciously observing and thinking about what is going on in the classroom, the more likely you are to begin to behave like this automatically and build up a stock of information that can be used to plan future action.

(8) Being open and honest

Control will be easier to achieve if you are open and honest with yourself and with senior staff about whatever difficulties you are having. This has already been discussed in some detail in the first chapter, but it is important enough to repeat, more briefly, here. The willingness and ability to be honest with yourself will prevent you from falling into the trap of denying that problems exist, for example redefining chaos as lively self-expression. Equally important is being open with colleagues, including senior staff. Without such openness, valuable support and advice cannot be obtained. If a problem is to be solved, it has to be acknowledged. Discussing control with senior colleagues before difficulties arise is an aid to openness, as it is easier to seek advice when you feel confident that your seniors will be supportive, as they should be. Remember that you are not alone— virtually all teachers have had problems with control. And remember, above all, that it is unethical and unprofessional to conceal such difficulties, as to do so will be to the detriment of your pupils' learning and general well-being.

(9) Thinking positively about yourself

Part of having good control is having the respect of your pupils. This is unlikely to be forthcoming unless you respect yourself, that is, as the jargon goes, that you have a positive self-concept. What can be done to achieve this with respect to your teaching? Firstly, do not dwell on your real or supposed inadequacies. Identify them and plan how to deal with them. Think also of your strengths—one of which is now your resolve to acknowledge and deal with your difficulties. The positive regard of others will help, so make the most of supportive colleagues, and of your friends and relatives—don't be tempted to neglect them as you spend too much time dwelling on your problems.

Another aspect of being positive about yourself is to make sure you don't neglect your own physical and mental health. This is not only in your own interests—it is to your pupils' benefit as well. If you come to school each day fit, lively and cheerful, this is far better for them than if you are tired and depressed. So avoid overwork—if you are regularly working more than two hours over the set school day (as many teachers do) this is probably too much. Have at least one day at the weekend completely free of school work and concerns, and maintain your other interests. Don't feel guilty about time spent on social, recreational and intellectual pursuits—they will make you a more relaxed, rounded and interesting person, more stimulating to

'Don't feel guilty about time spent on social, recreational and intellectual pursuits . . .'

pupils and more able to keep the problems of teaching in general (and control in particular) in proportion.

These then are the personal qualities which I believe are particularly relevant to class control. As already stated, they are put forward not as a description of the paragon you must be, but simply as a list of qualities likely to make control easier to achieve. As I hope I have already made clear, I do not mean to suggest that each of these qualities will be possessed by a teacher on an all-or-nothing basis, rather that each will be possessed to a certain degree, and that, generally, the greater the degree the better (although being too determined, too detached or too confident will bring their own problems). Moreover, most of them are capable of development with experience and certainly can be more clearly presented to pupils in the ways I have suggested.

The main points of this chapter

- Whatever control techniques are used, their success or failure will partly depend on the kind of person pupils perceive the teacher as being, and what they think she feels about them.

- Possession of certain personal qualities (listed below) will make it more likely that a teacher will be able to achieve good control.

- **Liking pupils and enjoying their company** can be developed by taking an interest in pupils' favourite music, sport, etc., by participating in extra-curricular activities, engaging in open and honest discussion and bringing humour, fun and play into classwork.

- **Believing in the value of learning** helps a teacher to persist in her efforts to achieve good control, in the knowledge that learning will make pupils better people in important ways and improve their life chances.

- **Being determined to succeed** also helps a teacher to persist when difficulties are encountered and can be fostered by focusing on the long-term benefits for pupils and teacher of overcoming present problems.

- **Being calm and relaxed** (or seeming to be so) can be aided by deliberately slowing movement and speech, trying to see the funny side of difficult situations and by sharing experiences of problems with supportive colleagues.

- **Being a little detached** emotionally from pupils helps a teacher to feel less annoyed and personally hurt by their misbehaviour.

- **Being confident** (or appearing to be so) means that a teacher is less likely to be challenged by pupils, and will develop through experience and being relaxed, a little detached and well prepared with regard both to work and possible misbehaviour.

- **Being thoughtful and analytical** about classroom behaviour allows a teacher to learn from observation what events and situations are likely to lead to misbehaviour.

- **Being open and honest** with herself and with senior colleagues about control difficulties helps a teacher to accept and face up to them and to seek support when appropriate.

- **Thinking positively about yourself** is necessary if you want your pupils to do the same, and involves identifying and dealing with your inadequacies, focusing on your strengths and taking care not to neglect friends and relatives or your physical and mental well-being.

Discussion questions

1. Taking each one of the nine personal qualities in turn, how important do you think it is for good control and to what extent do you think you now possess it? Which ones are your main problem areas? If you are discussing this in a group, which are the most common problem areas? Why do you think these are the most common?

2. How helpful and practicable in your view is the advice given here on how to develop or more clearly present each quality? How else might you set about improving yourself in these respects?

3

ORGANISATIONAL AND INTERPERSONAL STRATEGIES

It is now time to turn to the question 'What should I do to cope with misbehaviour?' I intend to answer this question in two ways. First, on the grounds that prevention is better than cure, I intend in this chapter to deal with various organisational and other 'background' activities and strategies that will help to create a climate in which misbehaviour is less likely to occur. Second, in the chapters which follow, I shall move on to describe a systematic approach aimed more directly at encouraging the good behaviour that occurs in classrooms and discouraging the bad.

However successful teachers are at controlling misbehaviour, all of them would prefer it never to occur in the first place. While such a perfect state of affairs is not possible, it is certainly possible to reduce the incidence of misbehaviour by creating a classroom climate, in terms of pupil and teacher attitudes and ways of working, that reduces reasons, opportunities and excuses for misbehaviour to a minimum. In achieving such a regime, a number of what might be called preventative strategies can be of help. These can be divided, for convenience, but with some overlap, into two categories: organisational strategies and interpersonal strategies.

Organisational strategies

(i) Organising work

In the early days with any class, and for as long as is necessary with a difficult class, misbehaviour can be minimised by taking steps to make sure that pupils' work is clearly within their capabilities and that it does not demand complex interactions by pupils or the use of complex resources. In other words, at this stage, management of behaviour is the priority, and simple behaviour is easier to manage than complicated behaviour. Individual work will generally offer fewer opportunities for misbehaviour than group work; groups of two will offer fewer opportunities than groups of three, and so on. As pupils prove themselves able to work sensibly and behave well, they should be allowed to take part in more complex activities. When introducing such work, it is generally better to start one or two groups working together while others work individually, awaiting their turn, which will come when they have proven themselves ready for it.

In a classroom where the work is really well-organised, no pupil will ever be able to say, justifiably, 'I don't know what to do', or 'I have nothing to do', for if either of these situations arises, misbehaviour is likely. How can such a classroom be achieved? First, clear instructions to pupils about their tasks are crucial. These should be given on an individual, group or class basis as appropriate, in straightforward language, repeated as necessary, and pupils (especially anyone who seems inattentive) should be questioned to make sure they have understood. Whenever possible, a short version of the instructions should be written on a board or card and displayed. Second, all pupils should always have more than enough work to keep them going. A help here is to make sure each pupil has individual long-term ongoing tasks (e.g. an individual project, a novel to read, story to write, strip cartoon to draw) so that he has always something to get on with should he forget what he is meant to be doing (or become 'stuck') when teacher help is not available. This means he has no

'Some children, often deliberately, spend a large part of their day queueing.'

reason or excuse to join a queue for the teacher's attention. Some children, often deliberately, spend a large part of their day queueing. This is a great waste of their time, as well as providing an opportunity for misbehaviour in the queue, and you would be well advised to allow 'queues' of no more than one pupil at any time.

A frequent occasion for misbehaviour is when pupils come into the classroom after breaks. Such misbehaviour can be much reduced if you make sure that they always have work to get on with at these times, without the need for guidance from the teacher.

From a control point of view, the main objective in organising work is to keep pupils busily engaged in legitimate activities, all of the time. If you can achieve this, or even come close to it, there will be little or no opportunity for misbehaviour.

(ii) Organising resources

In primary schools, and in most secondary school subjects, pupils' activities involve the use of resources of different kinds, such as paper, books, mathematical materials, scientific equipment, and so on. When the teacher is giving a lesson or demonstration, resources also play a part. The efficient storage and use of resources is necessary in creating a classroom atmosphere in which misbehaviour is relatively unlikely to occur, for the movement and pupil interaction involved in finding and using resources is a frequent source of trouble. The aims must be to minimise the movement and to make the pupil interaction as orderly as possible. What can the teacher do to achieve this?

First, with regard to storage, you should organise your resources as follows. Everything should have its own permanent place, and should be returned there after use. These places should be labelled to help pupils in returning items. The organisation of storage space should be logical, in that materials likely to be needed at the same time should be stored together, and materials likely to be in frequent use should be in the most accessible places. Items to which pupils are not supposed to have free access should be in inaccessible places, kept locked if possible. When particular sets of materials are required for intensive use, these should be brought out in advance to a convenient place. As far as is possible, materials should be obtained and returned by pupils, freeing the teacher to supervise. To avoid confusion, particular pupils should be entrusted with fetching and returning materials, rather than a free-for-all allowed. Sometimes it is appropriate to give particular responsibilities to particular pupils on a long-term basis, but favouritism should, of course, be avoided.

Second, the resources provided should always be adequate, in both quantity and quality, for the tasks to be carried out. If there are not, say, sufficient stop-watches for eight groups of four children carrying out a particular activity, it is better from a behaviour point of view to have only four groups working at a time on this activity, rather than to have two groups vying for the use of one stop-watch, for in situations like this pupils who have no intention of misbehaving can often end up squabbling simply due to their keenness to get on with the task. Quality of resources is also important. Teachers, partly because of schools' lack of finance, are frequently encouraged to produce home-made resource materials, and many excellent and ingenious devices result. While this is highly praiseworthy, home-made materials which are not fit for the task are counter-productive from a behaviour point of view. They either break or fail to work properly, resulting in pupil frustration (or hilarity) and consequent misbehaviour. Home-made materials should therefore be tested to make sure they do their job and are robust enough before they are given to pupils.

The use of resources by the teacher in a lesson is also a potential source of misbehaviour. These should be obtained (or made) well in advance, should work properly and be to hand when the lesson takes place. If something is forgotten, or fails to work properly, you are likely to become flustered and lose confidence with obvious adverse effects on the lesson, while the pupils are likely to be distracted or amused, with the consequent possibility of misbehaviour.

The largest resources in the classroom are the items of furniture and the space itself. Generally, you should try to use this space, including work surfaces, in ways appropriate to the tasks in hand. For example, if pupils are working with large sheets of paper, this is usually better not done on tables, where overlaps, bumping and disagreement are likely, but on the floor, with furniture rearranged, and pupils as spread out as possible (while leaving gangways for others to pass).

Normally, unless the work being undertaken is of a genuinely co-operative nature, pupils should be as well spaced out as possible. Sitting tightly bunched round a table is a very inappropriate situation for independent work. The tables in most types of classroom can be fairly readily moved by all but the youngest pupils into different arrangements for different types of work. Pupils need to be taught how to do this shifting, of course, otherwise chaos and misbehaviour will result, but learning to make the changes can be made a game, with different groups set different tasks and the teacher supervising, timing and judging the pupils' efforts. Three basic arrangements shown in the diagram below have proved useful over the years.

A is, of course, the most common present-day arrangement and many teachers keep their classrooms permanently like this. It is the most suitable layout for small group co-operative work, such as discussion, model-making, etc., but it is unsuitable for whole-class lessons or discussions (many children spend long periods of time sitting in a twisted position to see the teacher) and for individual work, where it leads to a great deal of copying and interference with other children's work. B is the best layout for individual work and C for whole-class lessons and discussions. It is not sensible, of course, to be changing the layout every half-hour, but one or two changes per day should not take an inordinate time, once the children have learned how to make them, and will repay the effort. Primary teachers, who normally have the same class all day, are more likely to find it practicable to change layouts. However, as a secondary English teacher, I can remember regularly making two shifts with a class of 42 first-year pupils within a period of 45 minutes, in order to move from whole-class discussion to small group co-operative writing and then to improvisation, for which all the desks were pushed together to clear a space. These pupils were not exceptional in any way, other than perhaps being keen on what we were doing. The secret of this small success was that I had carefully worked out the best ways to make the transitions and taught the pupils step-by-step how to carry out the procedures.

If you decide to use tables or desks in this flexible way, a disadvantage will be that each pupil will no longer have his own fixed place, which primary pupils especially seem to like. To compensate for this loss, it is important that each primary pupil should be given his own permanent place to keep his belongings, and,

Seating Plans

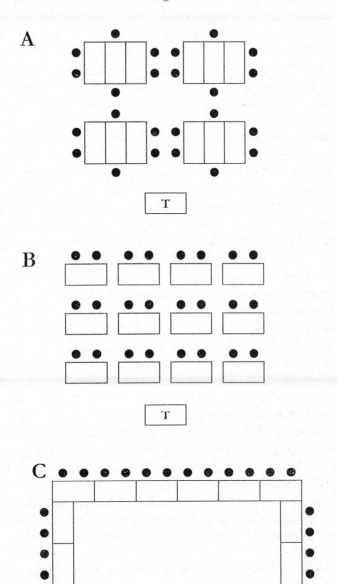

as far as is compatible with the work in hand, a regular position in each of the layouts. It is also desirable to start each day with the same layout. Although I am convinced that the use of different furniture layouts is desirable from a control point of view, it is crucial that the transitions are orderly. If you feel that you or your pupils are unlikely to be able to make the changes in an orderly manner, then it is better not to try, as the potential for misbehaviour is great. Later on, when you feel you have better control, will be a more suitable time to introduce this flexibility.

A final point about the use of space concerns types of activity. Try to keep activities which might interfere with each other as physically far apart as possible. Extreme and general examples of this are noisy and quiet activities and clean and messy activities. Much misbehaviour arises when children engaged in one sort of activity are in close proximity to others engaged in an incompatible one. Indeed, it is probably better to have such activities separated by time rather than space, but this, of course, is not always possible.

(iii) Establishing rules

Misbehaviour is behaviour which teachers don't want. Therefore every teacher who accepts that pupils sometimes misbehave must have rules in her mind, though she might think of these as 'standards' or 'expectations'. For pupils to learn not to break rules, they must obviously learn what the rules are. For many pupils, most of the time, the simple clear knowledge that there are rules against various kinds of behaviour means they are far less likely to behave in these ways. Establishing rules in the classroom is therefore an essential preventative measure in the teacher's campaign to reduce misbehaviour.

Some teachers are wary of making rules explicit with a new class, arguing that this will constitute a challenge to some pupils to break them, and that it is better to wait until a rule is broken, resulting in something going wrong (such as disruption to learning or damage to materials) before admonishing the pupils involved, pointing out the harm done and the need for the rule which is then laid down for the future. There is one main problem with this approach, which is that the single most important purpose of some rules is to ensure the safety of the pupils. It is simply not acceptable, for example, to wait until someone is hurt before introducing a rule about running in the classroom. Also, if some pupils regard rules as a challenge, it is unclear why this should be different if they are introduced one by one rather than all at once. It is sometimes argued, of course, that with the one by one approach, pupils appreciate the need for the rule, but this can be achieved in other ways such as by explanation.

I believe rules should be introduced early and explicitly. They should be as few as possible, as reasonable as possible and as positive as possible. Keeping them as few as possible means that pupils will find it easier to learn and remember them, and with fewer rules, there will be fewer occasions when a rule is broken. Making them as reasonable as possible means pupils are more likely to accept them as necessary and to see the rules and the teacher as being fair. Making them as positive as possible means that they actually guide pupils to behave as required rather than merely ban certain kinds of misbehaviour, thereby putting mischievous ideas into some heads. A final rule for rules is that pupils should be involved in their introduction. This can be done in a range of ways, from, at the one end of the participation spectrum, simply telling and displaying rules and engaging pupils in a discussion about why each is necessary, to, at the other end, presenting pupils with the problem (e.g. How can we make sure no-one gets hurt?) and leading them to produce a rule or rules to deal with it.

Whatever rules you produce must, of course, be in line with school policy. If you are in any doubt you must consult senior staff, because your rules can and will be broken and you may have to call upon senior staff for support if a pupil refuses to accept your authority. If your rule is not in line with school policy, you cannot, of course, expect support.

What rules should you have in your classroom? It is difficult to suggest a definitive set, given different schools' expectations and the different extents to which teachers will wish to involve pupils in their formulation, but leaving aside whole-school rules, such as those concerned with attendance, uniform, etc., here is a set to provide food for thought. It is suitable, in my view, for primary and younger secondary pupils.

(1) When you come into the classroom in the morning or after breaks, go straight to your place and sit there, ready to start work.

(2) When the teacher or a pupil is talking to the class or group, everyone listens.

(3) In a class lesson or discussion, put up your hand and wait until you're called by the teacher before speaking.

(4) Walk (don't run) in the classroom.

(5) Talk (don't shout) in the classroom.

(6) Always be polite and behave sensibly.

This is quite a short list, easy to learn, and each rule is easy to justify. All are positive instructions. Rule (1) can help to avoid a great deal of misbehaviour that can arise in the confusion of getting everyone into the classroom and settled. If your regime is such that pupils always have work to be getting on with, it can be amended so as to require them to make a start on it. It is, incidentally, a good idea for the teacher to position herself near the entrance to her classroom or area as pupils arrive. This allows her to control the flow of pupils and also makes pupils aware that they are entering territory where norms different from those of the playground apply.

Rules (2) and (3) seem necessary to me for civilised discussion. Before radio and TV began to broadcast from the House of Commons, I used to explain to pupils that even MPs had to wait politely for their turn to speak, a justification sadly no longer available, but, generally speaking, pupils (unlike MPs) see the need for these rules and are willing to abide by them. Rules (4) and (5) are necessary for safety and to avoid chaos, whose main classroom ingredients are too much noise and movement. Rule (6) covers everything else you might want, thus keeping the list short. Any unusual misbehaviour will be ruled out by this one, obviating the need to have rules about such things as climbing out of windows and the possibility of a certain type of pupil arguing that he has not done anything wrong as there is no specific rule against his behaviour.

If you have rules like these, carefully thought out with your school, classroom and pupils in mind, in line with school policy and clearly communicated to pupils who have had some involvement in their production, misbehaviour will be lessened. Also, when it does occur, it will be clearer to the pupils and yourself that it is unacceptable and that action will have to be taken to deal with it.

So much for organisational strategies which can help to lessen the incidence of misbehaviour. As stated earlier there are also a number of other strategies, which can be loosely grouped together as 'interpersonal'.

Interpersonal strategies

(i) Making pupils accountable

One crucial factor in determining how well any particular pupil will behave is how accountable that pupil feels in the classroom, that is, the extent to which he feels that what he does matters to the teacher, and that, if he misbehaves, this will be noticed and he will be brought to account for it. A great help to the teacher in enhancing pupils' feelings of accountability is getting to know them as individual persons. You should get to know pupils' names as quickly as possible, and as much as you can about their interests, opinions, likes and dislikes, brothers and sisters, and so on. As a pupil begins to believe he is a real person to you, he becomes less likely to feel anonymous and to engage in irresponsible misbehaviour directed at the teacher not as a person but as a symbol of adult authority. Getting to know your pupils should also involve trying to see things from their point of view, in other words trying to be understanding about their misbehaviour. This does not, of course, mean being indulgent with misbehaviour, but it will make it more likely that you can successfully reason with pupils about it. Thinking back to when you were a pupil at the same stage, and how you felt when teachers acted in particular ways, can be a great help. Don't forget that you had about twelve years of classroom experience before you ever started teacher education, and it would be very odd if you hadn't learned a great deal about classroom behaviour and misbehaviour from this time.

'The greater the number of pupils you have, of course, the more difficult it is to get to know them as individuals . . .'

The greater the number of pupils you have, of course, the more difficult it is to get to know them as individuals (the primary teacher has a great advantage here over the secondary teacher), but a determined effort to do this will pay real dividends. Once I heard a friend's child complain that, after one year at secondary school, only two of his teachers actually knew his name. I'm sure this is an extreme case, but put yourself, for a moment, in this pupil's position. Will he feel that his well-being and progress matter to his teachers? Will he feel that it matters if he misbehaves? In such a school, it is hardly surprising if pupils sometimes act as though they are part of an anonymous, unaccountable mob, and their teachers are not really people but simply agents of repression.

More directly, to make pupils feel accountable teachers have to monitor their work and behaviour. With regard to work, this means checking carefully that tasks set are actually undertaken, that written work is submitted and is of an acceptable standard, that marking is carried out properly, that records are kept so that any late or forgotten homework is checked up on, and so on. These things are important from the point of view of pupils' progress, of course, but also help to establish in pupils this feeling of accountability, the feeling that 'What I do or don't do matters'.

With regard to behaviour, the teacher should try to create in pupils the feeling that if they misbehave, this will be noticed and appropriate action taken. Even if there is no particular fear of punishment, most pupils are unlikely to misbehave if they believe they will be caught. To achieve this, you need, firstly, to get into the habit, as far as is practicable, of monitoring the behaviour of the whole class all the time. In the same way as an experienced driver checks his mirrors frequently without thinking about it, teachers who have good control constantly glance about the room and are aware of everything that is going on, even when they are engaged in discussion with one or a small group of pupils. Just like the driver's mirror technique, this needs to be done in a conscious way until it becomes automatic.

Ideally, pupils should come to feel that you have eyes in the back of your head, that you will be aware of all bad behaviour, and that there is therefore no point in misbehaving. A tactic which helps to create this belief is deliberately not to mention some non-extreme, furtive piece of misbehaviour when you first actually notice it, but to delay a little and comment on it when you are literally looking the other way: 'Why, Darren, have you had your shoes and socks off for the last five minutes?'

How the teacher moves about the classroom is another important determinant of success in monitoring behaviour. Ideally, your line of sight should include as many pupils for as much of the time as possible. This means, for example, that when moving round the room you should keep to the perimeter as much as possible, so that you are facing all or most of the class. When working with a corner group, you should place yourself at their outside corner, rather than turn your back on the class. It is important also not to get so involved with an individual pupil or group that you forget about the rest. If you find you have a tendency to do this, you must make a deliberate effort to look up every minute or so and consciously look round the class. Again, with time, this should become automatic.

It is best, as far as possible, never to leave pupils unattended; nor, until they have earned the privilege by good behaviour, to allow groups or individuals to work in unsupervised areas of the school. (Never, incidentally, do this without prior consent from senior staff.) Inevitably, however, you will have to leave pupils unattended on occasion. Such absences should be as short as possible, and pupils should be put on their honour not to misbehave. A useful training tactic is to leave very briefly and return unexpectedly, so that pupils don't get the feeling that your departure necessarily means they will have a long unsupervised spell. However, keep a sense of proportion about leaving pupils unsupervised—it would be rather surprising and even sad if a large group of children left to their own devices did not engage in a little monkey business. When returning from an absence from the classroom, it is a good idea to give the door handle a good rattle before entering. The behaviour will immediately improve, you can smile approvingly at your sensible class as you enter, and you will be less likely to need to remonstrate with anyone.

Pupils have to be kept alert and accountable in the course of lessons, as well as in their general work and activities. In discussions, avoid allowing the same few pupils to make most of the contributions. Asking for hands to be raised before choosing a pupil to answer shows how many are involved, and allows a range of pupils to be chosen and non-participants to be addressed. Asking sometimes for group, rather than individual responses (e.g. 'Hands up those who think X') also helps to maintain whole-group participation. Avoid anything which encourages pupils to switch off, e.g. getting pupils to answer in turns or concentrating on one group (or individual) in a whole-class activity.

Transition points, e.g. changing from a whole-class discussion or lesson to group activities, are times when pupils' attention and sense of accountability can lapse, as pupils suddenly feel no longer under direct supervision. Transitions therefore have to be carefully managed. With a new (or difficult) class it is probably wise to break up the class group by group with clear instructions to each group as to where to go and what to do, and to wait for each group to settle before moving to the next one. Unintentional 'transitions', that is interruptions to the flow of a lesson or set of activities are also times when pupils' attention can lapse. With careful planning, some of these can be eliminated (for example, make sure all 'business' matters, like registers, lunch-money, etc., are dealt with at the proper time), but there will always be interruptions over which individual teachers have little control, with consequent adverse effects on pupils' attention and involvement.

Some general points about getting and keeping the attention of the class can be made. One golden rule is not to begin talking to the class as a group until all pupils are silent and attentive. Most teachers find it useful to have a definite clear signal that class attention is required. A loud handclap is quite common and, although less popular, a bell, buzzer or chime can be very effective. These are all preferable to simply raising your voice, which can seem like (and often becomes) shouting, with its associations of annoyance and stress. If some pupils fail to come to attention (unlikely with a good loud, repeated signal) it is usually best to direct a remark at one or two, rather than at the whole class, and to maintain a pleasant attitude. ('David is so keen on his work that he hasn't heard me.') When attention is focused like this, other pupils become interested in what is to happen to the central character and watch and listen, that is, pay attention. This focusing technique, incidentally, is also the appropriate tactic for the teacher's nightmare situation, that is when the whole class is in chaos. Rather than try to quell the mob, it is better to focus on one miscreant, at random if necessary, and bring him, in as dramatic a fashion as possible, to the front of the room. Normally, the other pupils will fall silent to see what will happen, thus restoring order. Once this has occurred, nothing very extreme needs to happen to the pupil, unless, of course, his behaviour was really outrageous.

A final general point about getting and keeping pupils' attention is that it is highly desirable to get pupils to appreciate the purpose of and justification for your insistence that they keep alert and involved at all times, i.e. that it is for their benefit, so that they will always know what is going on and what they have to do.

To conclude this interpersonal section there are some additional points that can be dealt with much more briefly.

(ii) Avoid blaming or castigating the whole class

Seldom, if ever, is a whole class at fault, so it is both unfair and unproductive to engage in recriminations as if it was. The innocent will be antagonised and tempted to band together with the guilty if you regard them all as such, rapidly creating group solidarity against the teacher. A far better general line to take with an unruly class is, 'Some of you are letting us all down'.

(iii) Avoid nagging

Don't go on and on moralising about misbehaviour, on an individual, group or class basis. Take whatever action is needed and move on. Someone has misbehaved, but it has been dealt with, now you are friends again. Nagging pupils, or going into a huff with them, will produce resentment from them, consequent further misbehaviour and an unhappy atmosphere. Try to remember your pupils are only children, and misbehaviour, though it has to be stopped, is not something to agonise over.

(iv) Avoid threats you don't mean

If you threaten any consequence for misbehaviour, you must mean what you say and carry out the threatened course of action. If you don't, pupils will learn that you do not necessarily mean what you say, and needn't be taken seriously. Therefore don't issue any threats that you won't or can't carry out. ('I'll keep you in till 5 o'clock.')

(v) Be fair and consistent

Pupils have a strong sense of justice, and will quickly notice and resent unfair and inconsistent treatment. It is vital therefore to treat each pupil fairly and to be consistent in your response to misbehaviour. Sometimes this can be difficult, for example, when a normally well-behaved pupil transgresses, but it has to be done. If you occasionally feel exceptions have to be made to this rule, the reasons for this should be explained to the class.

(vi) Be punctual

If you expect pupils to be on time (and you should), then you must be punctual yourself. As well as this being necessary from an example-setting point of view, you will also find that a classic time for misbehaviour is when the teacher is late in arriving. It is also wise to be punctual in letting pupils go at break-times, as they are likely to feel resentful if they are last in the lunch queue, etc., through no fault of their own.

(vii) Avoid over-familiarity

It is your responsibility to be in charge of your pupils' work and behaviour. Therefore, although you should, of course, be friendly, you are not an equal, and should not allow pupils to become over-familiar with you. Details of your personal life and relationships are not their concern, and you should not be drawn into discussing them, especially in a frivolous way, although some aspects of your life (e.g. parent–child relationships) might be relevant to school and discussed in a serious way. Also, if you allow pupils to become familiar with you and feel like equals, they are likely to feel betrayed or resentful when the time comes when you have to require them to do as they are told by you.

If the preceding organisational and interpersonal strategies are employed, a great deal of misbehaviour will be prevented, which, as stated earlier, is a very desirable state of affairs. However, even in the best-run classrooms, misbehaviour will occur. The next two chapters will deal directly with how to cope with misbehaviour.

The main points of this chapter

- A range of organisational and interpersonal preventative strategies which will lessen the occurrence of misbehaviour can be employed in the classroom, as outlined below.
- Work can be organised in various ways which will reduce misbehaviour, such as the provision of straightforward work clearly within pupils' capabilities in the early days with a class, and by making sure that pupils always have some work to be getting on with.

- Efficient storage and use of resources in the classroom, minimising the pupil movement and interaction involved in finding and using resources, will also be beneficial.

- Classroom space and furniture should be utilised in the ways most appropriate to the tasks in hand; for example, different seating arrangements will reduce reasons and opportunities for misbehaviour during certain activities.

- Classroom rules in line with school policy should be established, as few, as reasonable and as positive as possible, and pupils should be involved in their introduction.

- The most important interpersonal strategy for reducing misbehaviour is to try to make pupils feel accountable for their actions.

- There are various ways of achieving this, for example getting to know pupils as individuals and forming relationships with them, and monitoring their work and general behaviour carefully.

- In particular, pupils should be made to feel accountable in the course of lessons by such strategies as interspersing requests for individual and group responses and avoiding concentration on a few members of the class.

- Transitions from one type of activity to another should be carefully managed as pupils' sense of accountability tends to falter when they do not feel under close supervision.

- Other interpersonal strategies which lessen the likelihood of misbehaviour include being fair, consistent and punctual and avoiding the tendency to blame the whole class when only some pupils deserve blame, nagging, over-familiarity and the making of unrealistic threats.

Discussion questions

1. In your teaching to date, how successful do you feel you have been in organising work and resources? What main

difficulties have you found, and what have been the consequences, in terms of pupil behaviour, of these?

2. Do you agree that different seating arrangements are suited
to different activities? What seating policy would you adopt?

3. How useful do you think the set of rules given in this chapter
is? What changes would you make?

4. Have you found any of the interpersonal strategies discussed
above difficult to follow in practice? Why?

4

A BEHAVIOURAL, REFLECTIVE, RELATIONSHIP (BRR) APPROACH

So far, I have dealt, first, with what I consider to be some fallacious answers to the problems of class control; second, with the kind of person a teacher should ideally try to be to reduce the likelihood of misbehaviour; and, third, with the kind of classroom regime and atmosphere which is most likely to help in achieving this goal. However, no matter how close a teacher and the atmosphere she creates come to these ideals, misbehaviour will still occur and action to deal with it will have to be taken. In my opinion, a teacher should have a well worked-out general strategy or approach to use in such circumstances; it is not likely that simply reacting to events as they occur, even against the background of being the right sort of person, and having the right sort of classroom atmosphere, will be effective.

In this chapter, I shall outline an approach which I think is likely to be successful for most teachers. It is a combination of elements of two approaches rooted in two different kinds of psychology often held to be incompatible, behaviourist and cognitive psychology. A brief account of the nature of the different approaches to classroom control that stem from these different viewpoints is therefore necessary before I go on to suggest how they can be profitably combined.

First, the **behavioural** approach. Traditional behavioural psychology embodies three basic ideas, as follows:

(i) Psychology should deal with observable behaviour, that is what people do and say, and not with things that cannot be observed and measured, such as thoughts, feelings and purposes.

(ii) Behaviour is learned, that is, it is a product of experiences the person has had, and it is possible for a person to stop behaving in certain ways, and to begin to behave in different ways, as a result of further experiences.

(iii) Changes in behaviour are governed primarily by the consequences of our actions. We tend to repeat behaviour which leads to consequences we desire, and not to repeat behaviour which leads to consequences which are undesired by us or unpleasant to us.

The teacher who applies these principles to classroom control will concentrate on pupils' behaviour, that is, what they do and say in the classroom, rather than spend time and effort thinking about their feelings or their reasons for misbehaving. Her general strategy will be as follows:

(i) Decide what is wanted in terms of pupil behaviour.

(ii) Apply behavioural techniques to increase desired behaviour.

(iii) Apply behavioural techniques to lessen undesired behaviour.

The main behavioural techniques available to teachers are reward, extinction and punishment. If a behaviour is followed by a reward, it is more likely to occur again. Behaviourists prefer the term 'reinforcer' to reward, principally because things that would normally never be thought of as rewards can have the effect of 'reinforcing' a behaviour, that is, making it more likely to recur. For instance, a teacher's reprimands to a pupil for silly behaviour in the classroom can have the effect of increasing the occurrence of such behaviour, in that the teacher's attention to him is acting as a reinforcer. He is seeking attention, and any attention is better than none to him, but neither teacher nor pupil would think of the reprimands as rewards. However, for our present purposes, the everyday term reward, rather than reinforcer, will be used. To a behaviourist, reward should be the main strategy for changing classroom behaviour. Rather than focus on misbehaviour, the teacher should identify desirable behaviour ('catch them being good', rather than bad), and encourage this by means of rewards of different kinds, applied systematically on either a group or an individual basis.

Misbehaviour, to the behaviourist, can be dealt with in different ways. First, if good behaviour which is incompatible with certain bad behaviour is established by reward, the bad behaviour, logically, cannot take place. For instance, if 'going straight to your place' after breaks is fully established, the communal area misbehaviour which previously occurred at this time will not now occur. Second, extinction of behaviour can be utilised. Extinction is the process whereby a behaviour that is no longer rewarded will occur less and less frequently, before finally disappearing. Applying this technique requires the teacher to identify the rewards that are keeping the misbehaviour going and eliminating them. This is not easy to do in the classroom, for reasons that will be discussed later. The third main behavioural way of dealing with misbehaviour is by punishment, that is, by arranging for something unpleasant to or undesired by the misbehaving pupil to happen to him after the misbehaviour. This makes the recurrence of the misbehaviour less likely. Behaviourist writers on classroom control tend to advocate a minor role (or no role at all) for punishment, regarding it as a very negative strategy. They much prefer reward, which guides pupils to good behaviour, to punishment, which merely stops misbehaviour. The term 'negative reinforcement' is sometimes used for punishment, but this is not strictly accurate. Reinforcement always increases the likelihood of behaviour, whereas punishment decreases it. Negative reinforcement, correctly, is the kind of 'reward' that is involved when something unpleasant is stopped or removed after the occurrence of desired behaviour. This has the effect of increasing the likelihood of the desired behaviour occurring again. For instance, making a pupil who is reluctant to work sit by himself is a punishment; letting him rejoin his group when he starts working properly is negative reinforcement.

A final point about the behavioural approach is that the teacher is expected to be systematic in her approach. Behaviour is observable and therefore measurable. It is not satisfactory, for example, simply to reward certain behaviours in ways that seem appropriate and to hope that control will improve. The thoroughgoing behavioural teacher will identify the target behaviour precisely, and, by observation and counting, obtain a 'baseline' or initial level of occurrence for it. Then the behavioural technique will be applied and further observation and measurement carried out to detect any change.

To sum up, the behavioural approach is a matter of discouraging undesired behaviour, and, especially, encouraging desired behaviour, in a systematic way. The steps involved are: (i) identifying a target behaviour to be changed; (ii) obtaining, by observation, a measure of the frequency with which it occurs, thus establishing a baseline; (iii) applying an appropriate behavioural technique (usually a reward of some kind) to effect the change; and (iv) measuring the change in the incidence of the target behaviour.

The second of the main approaches mentioned earlier is the **cognitive** approach. This approach comes from a psychological viewpoint quite different from, indeed opposed to, the behavioural one. From this viewpoint, the idea of disregarding pupils' thoughts, feelings, motives, etc., and concentrating simply on their behaviour is regarded as folly, for it is thoughts, feelings and motives that are held to be the essence of the person. Behaviourism is therefore seen as so narrow as to be of little use in understanding people and what they do. In particular, in thinking about and trying to cope with the problems of class control, a teacher would be encouraged, from a cognitive viewpoint, to try to see the classroom situation from the pupils' point of view. The cognitive psychologist sees the pupil as a person trying to make sense of the world around himself, and trying to deal with it in ways that contribute to his survival, well-being and development. If he sees what the teacher has created around him as relevant to his concerns and likely to help him to develop in ways he likes and thinks are important, then he is likely to co-operate in the work of the class. But if he sees what is going on as worrying, or boring, or irrelevant to his concerns and how he wants to develop, then he is unlikely to co-operate. It is therefore clear that 'making the work interesting' to pupils is seen as crucial in this approach, and the teacher who is having difficulties would be advised to consider what it is about what she is teaching, or how she is teaching it, that is responsible for her failure to connect with the pupils. In trying to answer this question, she would be urged to try to see things from the pupils' point of view, bearing in mind their age, interests, home background, general ability, existing skills and knowledge, etc., and to make appropriate changes in what and how she is teaching.

Another central aspect of the cognitive approach is the importance it attaches to the influence on a pupil's behaviour of his self-concept, that is his view of himself as a person, and, in particular, of his academic self-concept, that is, how he sees himself as a pupil and learner. From the cognitive viewpoint, this aspect of the self-concept is very important in determining how a pupil behaves when he is engaged, or is supposed to be engaged, in school work. If he has a positive academic self-concept, he regards himself as a person likely to be able to undertake the task set for him and to succeed reasonably well. He is therefore likely to tackle the task in a realistic and positive way, in other words, he will make a genuine effort to cope with it, feeling that such an effort is likely to be worthwhile because his attempt is likely to be fruitful. With such an attitude and behaviour, he is unlikely to engage in misbehaviour. However, many pupils have negative academic self-concepts. Their expectations are of difficulty and failure, and engaging in a set task

'How many adults persist with a sport or leisure activity for which
they show little talent?'

with such expectations will produce feelings of anxiety and unhappiness. Such pupils are likely to try to avoid such feelings,
naturally enough. This can be done in different ways. A pupil
might directly refuse to undertake the task; he might find excuses not to attempt it; he might merely pretend to engage in it;
he might engage in it, but set himself a very low target (for
example, attempting only the first few and easiest maths examples in an exercise). All of these are likely to be seen by the
teacher as 'not trying', with consequent potential for conflict. No

one likes failure and difficulty (how many adults persist with a sport or leisure activity for which they show little talent?), but teachers, who have all been relatively successful academically, often find it difficult to appreciate just how dispiriting it is for pupils to have to persist day in and day out in activities where they feel doomed to failure. 'Not trying' is therefore often a means to avoid failing, rather than defiance of the teacher's wishes.

Another way in which the pupil with a poor academic self-concept can avoid coming to grips with his work is by making his feelings about himself open to others—'I can't do it, I'm too stupid, there's no point in me trying'. This can also be exasperating to the teacher, but less so than defiance, avoidance or minimal engagement, and can often induce in the teacher some admiration for the pupil for being 'honest', as well as sympathy for his difficulties. Perhaps most worrying from a control point of view, however, is the low self-concept pupil who not only shields himself from failure by refusing to engage in set work, but who, instead of blaming himself for this, blames the teacher, the school or adult society in general. The most common way of doing this is to decide that the work is boring and irrelevant, that the teacher is boring, incompetent and unfair, and that school and education in general are a waste of time. It makes matters worse if there is an element of truth in such views, even if the pupil's main reason for forming them is his own fear of failure. If a pupil, or a number of pupils feel like this, then misbehaviour is very likely to occur, in a form that will be extremely difficult to cope with.

What are the implications for class control of this analysis from a self-concept viewpoint? These are, in principle, fairly clear, if difficult to put into practice. The teacher's aim should be to improve the pupil's self-concept, both generally as a person, and, in particular, as a learner. To help enhance his general self-concept, the teacher has to get across the message that she genuinely values him as a person; that he is acceptable and worthwhile as a member of the class; that she likes his company and wants to help him. This can only be achieved through friendly interaction with pupils, and by taking a genuine interest in their ideas, opinions and work. As far as the pupil's academic self-concept is concerned, the main way towards improvement is to structure his work carefully so that he begins to experience success and to feel competent, albeit at a low level at first. If this can be achieved, he should become progressively more willing to engage in the work. If a large group or whole class of pupils has much the same needs, this gradation of work is likely to meet with some success, but if only one or two pupils are involved, their desire not to be obviously 'behind' their peers can make them very unwilling to engage in work within their capabilities.

The above brief accounts of the behavioural and cognitive approaches should have made it clear why they are often held to be incompatible, and in their extreme forms they probably are. However, I believe that elements from each can be combined to produce an approach which is more in tune with teachers' everyday perceptions of pupils and classrooms, and therefore more likely to be acceptable and successful in practice, than either approach by itself.

The first step in formulating such a combined approach is to identify the elements of each of the two constituent approaches which seem useful and compatible with one another, and those which seem incompatible, unnecessary or unproductive. This can be done by comparing and contrasting the two approaches under three headings: first, the significance of misbehaviour in each (in two senses of significance, i.e. importance and meaning); second, the kind of relationships between teacher and pupil in each; and third, the techniques for improving control suggested by each.

1. The significance of misbehaviour

In the behavioural approach, behaviour and misbehaviour are all-important. Whatever is in the hearts and minds of pupils, it is what they do and say that constitutes order or disorder, and which has to be encouraged or discouraged. From a cognitive viewpoint, behaviour is seen more as an indicator of whether such things as motives and self-concepts are in a healthy state. Misbehaviour in itself is therefore mainly a symptom of a problem, rather than the problem itself. If the underlying problems are dealt with then the symptom is likely to disappear. Which is the right side to be on here? As will be apparent from a previous chapter, I strongly believe that misbehaviour must not be left to 'sort itself out' while underlying problems of one sort or another are addressed. If this is done, work and learning will be subject to long-term disruption, which simply cannot be allowed in the classroom. Having said this, however, the notion of behaviour as the be-all and end-all, and consequent exclusion from consideration of such matters as motives and pupils' perceptions of events, seem equally wrong. In trying to stop misbehaviour and encourage good behaviour, the reasons why pupils engage in one or the other are often of importance, and it is surely far too narrow to restrict the consideration of possible reasons for their behaviour to the past consequences of pupils' actions, as the extreme behavioural approach does. To sum up, the 'combined' or compromise view I take here is that, from a control point of view, behaviour and misbehaviour are very important in themselves, and misbehaviour has to be directly and speedily addressed. However, in coping with misbehaviour, and encouraging good behaviour, pupils' motives, as well as other reasons for their behaviour, are of importance and must be taken into consideration.

2. The relationship between teacher and pupil

The roles of teacher and pupil and the teacher's attitude to the pupil are quite different in each approach. In the extreme behavioural approach, the teacher's role is a detached, mechanical, even manipulative one. The teacher simply defines the behaviour she wants, and arranges the consequences of the pupil's

actions so that desired behaviour becomes more likely and undesired behaviour less likely. The teacher takes on a role not
unlike that of a scientist with the pupils as the subjects in her
experiments, as she observes behaviour, establishes baselines,
measures changes, and so on. In the cognitive approach, on the
other hand, the quality of the human relationship between
teacher and pupils is all-important. Great stress is laid upon the
teacher trying to see things from the pupils' point of view (that
is, to empathise with them in the way that a counsellor does),
and upon trying to improve pupils' self-concepts by means of a
genuinely warm and positive attitude to them.

When contrasted like this, both of these models of teacher–pupil
relationships seem somewhat inappropriate to real-life teaching.
The behaviourist teacher does not seem like a normal human
being interacting with other human beings in anything like a
natural way, but like a scientist with her subjects, as suggested
previously, or a puppet-master. The cognitive teacher, on the
other hand, seems impossibly virtuous, warm, positive, caring
and understanding about all of her pupils, no matter how hor-
ridly they might behave towards her, and extremely non-
directive. As a model, the cognitive approach seems, perhaps,
more appropriate for a counsellor than a classroom teacher. A
compromise between the two extremes is necessary. As suggested in an earlier chapter, a little detachment is probably a
good thing for a teacher. The behavioural teacher above is too
detached, the cognitive one probably too involved. Genuine interest and human warmth towards pupils are highly desirable in
a teacher, but, from a control point of view, it is also clearly
necessary for the teacher to be 'in charge', and not just an adult
friend, helper, or counsellor.

3. Techniques for improving control

The behaviourist approach offers very clear guidance on techniques, which are relatively easy, at least in principle, to apply.
Concentrating on desired behaviour and encouraging it with

'The behaviourist teacher (seems) like a scientist with her subjects.'

rewards, while discouraging undesired behaviour where necessary by means of punishments of different sorts, is an attractively simple and direct strategy. The main techniques suggested by the cognitive approach, namely making the work interesting to pupils and endeavouring to improve pupils' self-concepts, are more general, more difficult to apply, much less clear-cut and seem likely to take a much longer time to have an impact on pupils' behaviour than rewards and punishments. However, both techniques seem worthwhile from a control point of view, as well as desirable from a general educational viewpoint. A compromise between the two approaches with regard to techniques does not necessarily involve a choice between the behavioural and cognitive ones. In my view the techniques are compatible. The more direct behavioural ones and the less direct cognitive ones can be applied by the same teacher with the same class; for instance, rewards of certain kinds can be used to build self-esteem. A compromise approach to control can involve both sets of techniques.

Before going on to list the elements of the two approaches that can be combined, it is necessary to invent a name for this compromise approach. The term **behavioural, reflective, relationship approach**, although clumsy, seems appropriate. It is behavioural because it acknowledges the importance of behaviour and misbehaviour and addresses them directly; it is reflective because, rather than addressing the problems of control in a mechanical, impersonal way, it stresses the need to reflect upon the thoughts, feelings, desires, needs and motives of pupils; and it is a relationship strategy because it requires the teacher to enter into genuine human relationships with pupils. The elements from the behavioural and cognitive approaches that comprise this BRR approach (an unfortunate acronym for an approach that requires a warm relationship) can now be listed.

(1) From the behavioural approach

(i) The teacher is in charge of, and responsible for, pupils' behaviour.

(ii) Behaviour is important in itself, and not just as a symptom of underlying problems.

(iii) Misbehaviour must be stopped as quickly as possible.

(iv) There should be an emphasis on the positive, i.e. encouraging good behaviour.

(v) Techniques directly aimed at changing behaviour, such as rewards and punishments, should be used.

(2) From the cognitive approach

(i) Pupils' purposes or motives in behaving well and badly are often important and must be taken into account.

(ii) The teacher must try to see things from the pupils' point of view, as well as her own.

(iii) The teacher must try to create warm, positive, genuine relationships with pupils.

(iv) Pupils' general and academic self-concepts have an important influence on their behaviour.

(v) The teacher must try to bring about positive changes in the self-concepts of misbehaving pupils.

(vi) Pupils will behave better if they are engaged in work they find interesting.

These principles seem to me to be useful and compatible and to form a sound basis for a balanced, directive yet humane approach to classroom control. Some aspects of the behavioural and cognitive approaches have been omitted: from the behavioural approach, the mechanical, impersonal way of regarding pupils' behaviour, the unwillingness to take pupils' purposes and feelings into account, and the 'teacher as experimenting scientist' role; from the cognitive approach, the tendency to relegate misbehaviour to the status of a symptom. 'Making the work interesting' as a means of achieving control has been relegated to the end of the list in view of what I have said earlier about it. While I regard it as a highly desirable educational aim, and as an aid to class control, I have already made clear, I hope, why I feel it should not be given anything like the primacy that the cognitive approach attaches to it.

The list above comprises the main principles of the BRR approach. How should it be put into practice? The next chapter addresses this question.

The main points of this chapter

● However successful a teacher is at being the kind of person and creating the kind of classroom atmosphere likely to produce good control, misbehaviour will always occur and a well worked-out general strategy to deal with it is necessary.

- An approach likely to be successful for most teachers can be formulated by combining elements of behaviourist and cognitive psychology.

- Traditional behaviourist psychology embodies the notions that observable behaviour should be the focus of concern, that behaviour is learned from experience and can be changed, and that behaviour is governed by its consequences.

- The three main behavioural techniques which can be used by teachers are reward, which makes behaviour more likely to recur, and punishment and extinction (absence of reward) which make behaviour less likely to recur.

- The behaviourist approach requires systematic identification and quantification of behaviour as well as the application of techniques to effect change.

- Cognitive psychology focuses on processes internal to the person, such as thoughts, beliefs and motives.

- Taking a cognitive approach to control involves the teacher in trying to see classroom situations from pupils' points of view and making sure that pupils see what they are asked to do as relevant to their concerns and in their interests.

- The cognitive view also stresses the importance of helping pupils to develop positive self-concepts or views of themselves as persons and learners.

- With a positive academic self-concept a pupil will see himself as likely to succeed with his work and make genuine efforts, whereas with a negative self-concept he is likely to expect failure and may try to avoid engaging in his work.

- The behavioural and cognitive approaches differ in the significance they attach to misbehaviour, the kind of relationships between teacher and pupil they imply and the control techniques they involve.

- In their extreme forms, the behavioural and cognitive approaches seem incompatible, but a selection of principles and techniques from both of them can be combined into a compromise approach.

- This approach can be called the **behavioural, reflective, relationship** approach because it addresses behaviour directly, it stresses the need for the teacher to reflect upon pupils' thoughts, feelings and motives, and it requires genuine human relationships between teacher and pupils.

Discussion questions

1. If you had to choose between the behavioural and cognitive approaches, with which would you be in most sympathy, and why? What in your view are the strongest and weakest points of each?

2. Do you agree that all eleven of the BRR principles are compatible with one another? If not, which ones do you think are in conflict?

5

PUTTING THE BRR APPROACH INTO PRACTICE

In chapter 4 I outlined the main features of an approach to control which draws from both behavioural and cognitive psychology—a behavioural, reflective, relationship approach. In this longer chapter, I shall attempt to describe how such an approach might be put into practice. Part of the cognitive influence on the BRR approach is embodied in the suggestions I have made in chapters 2 and 3 about what sort of personal and inter-personal attributes, attitudes and skills in a teacher are most conducive to good control. The first steps to take in applying this approach are therefore to try, as far as possible, to be the kind of teacher described in chapter 2 and to create the kind of class-room climate suggested in chapter 3. The main contribution of the behavioural viewpoint to the BRR approach is its advocacy of the use of rewards and punishments to bring about desired changes in behaviour, but here again there is a cognitive influence, in that the choices of rewards and punishments and of their mode of employment are made in the light of a cognitive interpretation of pupil and teacher behaviour.

Assume, for the moment, you are as near to a chapter 2 and 3 teacher as you can manage. You are starting (as a teacher, not a student on a short placement, when the best plan is to fall in at least initially with the class teacher's approach) with a new class or set of classes. How should you go about applying a BRR approach? The general strategy would be as follows.

Be firm, pleasant and 'in charge'. Early on, make it clear what your classroom rules are and why each is necessary, involving the pupils to a greater or lesser extent in their formulation, as previously described. Remember that your rules should be as few, as reasonable and as positive as practicable, and in line with school policy, so that support will be forthcoming from your senior staff if necessary. (This is quite likely to be the case, as some pupils will test you out, to see if you mean what you say.) Be prepared to employ punishments (details later) if rules are broken. The work you set, and the way you organise the class, should, early on, be chosen to facilitate good control, rather than to inspire or impress pupils, for, unless they are behaving well, they will be unlikely to take it seriously enough to be inspired or impressed. This means the work set should be straightforward from an organisational viewpoint, and clearly within pupils' capabilities. Within these limitations, it should, of course be as potentially interesting as possible. With a good class, this tight regime can be relaxed quite soon, but with a more difficult class, it should be firmly and consistently maintained until the classroom is clearly an orderly place, for some weeks if necessary.

Gradually, rewards (details later) should be introduced, to encourage good behaviour. As the occurrence of good behaviour increases, so, logically, the occurrence of misbehaviour will lessen, and with it the need for punishments, although it is unlikely that punishment could ever be abandoned entirely, as some behaviourists believe. As time goes on, a positive atmosphere created by rewards and concentration on good behaviour, rather than punishment and concentration on misbehaviour, will develop. Rewards can be aimed at particular problems (e.g. punctuality), or at general classroom behaviour if there seems to be a large number of problem areas. An attempt should be made to raise, progressively, the level of rewards being employed (see below). If this approach is persisted with, misbehaviour should decrease, good behaviour increase, and the pupils become, gradually, more orderly, happy and hardworking.

In the above bald outline, the BRR approach might seem overly behavioural. The cognitive influence comes into play again, however, when the teacher considers and makes decisions about the kind of rewards and punishments to use, and the ways to use them.

The use of rewards

To many teachers, it seems natural to think of good behaviour as merely what is to be expected and taken for granted. Rewards, if thought of at all by such teachers, are reserved for specially good behaviour, and punishment for behaviour less good than expected is seen as the main means of class control. One of the best aspects, in my opinion, of the behavioural viewpoint on control is the change it advocates to this attitude. Pupils' behaviour, however bad, is realistically accepted as the starting point, any improvement on which merits reward. In this way, as already stated, 'Catch them being good and reward them' replaces 'Catch them being bad and punish them'. The benefits of this change lie not only in the improvements in behaviour which can be achieved through it, but in the general positiveness of attitude which it induces in teachers towards their pupils. If you are actively looking for and focusing on good behaviour or improvements in behaviour in your pupils, rather than looking for misbehaviour, you are, of course, likely to be much nicer to them and perceived by them as liking them.

Another result of teachers' traditional disinclination to use rewards is that they often find it difficult to think of rewards that can be readily employed in the classroom, especially if they are struggling for control. If you are stressed and unhappy, not particularly liking or being liked by your pupils, who seem to be constantly squabbling and misbehaving, your classroom doesn't, on the face of it, seem to be a very fertile source of rewards. However, there are in fact many rewards potentially available to teachers. These have been described and categorised in various ways. For the list below, I have taken 'reward' in a wide sense, to include all the kinds of rewarding experiences that pupils might have in the classroom, and placed these in an order of educational desirability from 1 to 6.

Classroom rewards

(1) Intrinsic rewards

(2) Experience of success or making progress

(3) Other people's praise or approval

(4) Preferred activities

(5) Token rewards

(6) Tangible (including edible) rewards

What does each type of reward involve?

(1) Intrinsic reward is the most educationally desirable kind of reward. Ideally, teachers want all of their pupils to experience it in all of their work. By intrinsic reward is meant the pleasure and satisfaction that people sometimes get from the work or other activity that they are engaged in. For example, when a pupil is attempting a tricky maths problem, finding it interesting and a challenge and enjoying this, he is having a rewarding experience which will make him more likely to behave in this highly desirable way when he is set problems to tackle in the future.

(2) Experience of success or making progress is the next most desirable level. By this is meant, for example, the feeling of satisfaction that the above-mentioned pupil will obtain from getting the correct answer to the maths problem. Note that this is not the same thing as intrinsic reward, i.e. the pleasure derived from puzzling over the problem. Intrinsic reward is possible without success being achieved, and success is possible without intrinsic reward. However, the two will obviously often go together. All of us like to succeed, and getting things right,

completing an exercise satisfactorily and going on to the next one, and so on, can be quite potent motivators for pupils. Sadly, however, many school pupils have little experience of either intrinsic reward or success.

(3) Other people's praise or approval, in many forms (verbal, smiles, nods, etc.) can act as rewards in the classroom. Many teachers believe they use this type of reward frequently, and approval from other pupils is also a frequent and potent form of reward. The latter, of course, is not always used to reward behaviour desired by the teacher. Peer approval of bad behaviour is a powerful continuous influence in many classrooms and has to be stopped or at least lessened if improvements in general behaviour are to be achieved. The teacher's task here is to try to create situations in which peer approval is redirected from undesired (by the teacher) to desired behaviour.

(4) Preferred activities can be potent rewards. In general, the opportunity to engage in any preferred activity will serve as a reward for engaging in any less-desired activity. For instance, pupils can be allowed a few minutes free time at the end of a lesson if they have worked and behaved well. It is important to note that not only clearly recreational activities, such as games and free time, can serve as rewards, although these are obviously useful and should be employed. In fact, many aspects of normal school work are more desired than other aspects and can serve as rewards. The reward activity does not need to be highly attractive, just more attractive than the one for which it is being used as a reward. For example, if a primary pupil is finding his daily maths a grind, but is better at writing, then the chance to write a story if he perseveres with his maths will serve as a reward. In fact, even if the second activity is disliked, it can serve as a reward so long as it is less disliked than the first.

(5) Token rewards refer to all the kinds of points, stars, credits, etc., that teachers can use. These rewards are called tokens because they have no value in themselves, but represent something else that is valued. Sometimes teachers do this in a

'In general, the opportunity to engage in any preferred activity
will serve as a reward for engaging in any less-desired activity.'

concrete way; for example, five coloured stars can earn a gold
star, and three gold stars earn the chance to play a game or have
five minutes free time. Sometimes, however, token rewards have
value simply in that they represent success, or at least compara-
tive success (doing better than other individuals or groups) like
goals scored in a football match. Primary teachers, in particular,
can benefit from point or star systems based on groups, which
involve competition between groups and co-operation (and social
approval) within groups. Token systems (group or individual)
can only really work if all pupils or all groups see themselves as
actually being rewarded. This will not be the case if some individuals or groups fall far behind the others. The composition of

groups, and the criteria for allocating points, have to be such as to ensure a good degree of success for all.

(6) Tangible (including edible) rewards are, in my view, not really appropriate for use in ordinary schools with ordinary pupils. Tangibles (trinkets, small toys, sweets, etc.) have been used successfully in special schools with extremely difficult or disturbed children with whom higher levels of reward have been unsuccessful. In the ordinary school, however, it should not normally be necessary to go down to this level. This is not to say, of course, that there is any harm (other than dental) in a teacher giving young children a sweet as an occasional treat, but to use tangibles as rewards in any conscious or systematic way would not meet with approval in most schools. Having said this, however, it is salutary to remember that most adult work is rewarded by tokens, i.e. money, and the tangibles it buys.

Having outlined the different types of reward available, the next step is to try to establish a set of principles governing the different aspects of their use, such as criteria for selection of rewards for different situations. The influence of the cognitive viewpoint becomes significant here, as will be seen from the following guidelines.

1. Levels of reward

As previously stated, the higher levels of reward are educationally preferable. This means that before setting up, say, a token system, the teacher should have taken steps to see to what extent higher levels of reward might have been effective, by, for example, trying to offer success experience, ascertaining the effect of teacher praise, and so on. The term 'reinforcement overkill' has been used for the giving of rewards at a lower level than is necessary, and while this is, of course, to be avoided if possible, it is inevitable that teachers working with a whole class or large group will sometimes be guilty of it. For instance, if a reward of five minutes free time is given at the end of a lesson to all those who have finished a task on time, pupils who would have finished it anyway because they enjoyed it (intrinsic reward), and those who would have finished it because they generally get satisfaction from task completion (success experience), are being rewarded, by the free time, at a lower level than necessary. Is this harmful? Some writers on motivation have suggested that 'intrinsic motivation' (that is, doing something because you like it) is likely to be weakened or 'undermined' by lower level rewards. If this is the case, then whole-class or large group use of rewards would be potentially harmful, and changing behaviour by rewards would have to be carried out in a painstaking individualised way, matching rewards to each pupil's needs. Such an approach would be impracticable as a general classroom strategy.

In principle, the notion of undermining is plausible enough, in that a person who does something because he likes doing it seems likely to lose some of this motivation if he begins to be 'paid' for doing it by a reward at some lower level. That is, he might begin to see himself as doing it for the lower reward. However, if this principle were to be applied to everyday life, it would mean, for instance, that an enthusiastic teacher would enjoy teaching more if she were paid less, and even more if she were paid nothing at all. Also, a footballer would enjoy playing football less if he won cups or awards. Such examples of undermining seem less plausible than the principle, and, indeed, it has been suggested that lower-level rewards in school can actually increase intrinsic motivation, so long as the lower reward is seen by the pupil as an acknowledgement or symbol of doing well, rather than as payment for carrying out an activity. In using rewards, teachers should therefore always try to make it clear to pupils that lower-level rewards have this significance. Here the pupil's understanding of the meaning of the reward, which would have no place in a strict behavioural approach, is clearly of great importance.

2. Raising the level

An ongoing attempt should be made to raise the level of reward being used. This can be done by pairing or associating higher-level rewards with lower-level ones that are proving effective.

For instance, sometimes a pupil can move from level (3) (others' approval) to level (1) (intrinsic reward) in the following way:

Stage 1   John works hard: rewarded with peer approval for having earned his group a point by completing a set task (accompanied by feeling of 'I've finished this')

With repetition of Stage 1, 'finished feeling' (i.e. success experience) becomes a secondary reward by association with primary reward of social approval.

Stage 2   John works hard: rewarded by success experience (accompanied by intellectual engagement in the task)

With repetition of Stage 2, intellectual engagement (i.e. intrinsic reward) becomes a tertiary reward by association with secondary reward of success experience.

Stage 3   John works hard: rewarded by intrinsic reward.

While things will not always work out as well as this, it is often productive, and certainly does no harm, for the teacher to try to ensure that potential higher-level rewards accompany lower-level ones so that pupils have the chance of forming such associations.

3. Frequency of rewards

A simple rule, well-established by behaviourists, concerns the frequency with which rewards, for maximum effectiveness, should be given. When a desired behaviour is in the process of being established, ideally every occurrence of it should be rewarded, but once it is established, occasional reward is more effective in maintaining it. Careful monitoring of the occurrence of a particular desired behaviour, and painstaking scheduling (as it is called) of rewards is more practicable in the behaviourist laboratory than in the classroom, but within the limits of practicability, teachers can apply this principle. Simply, when trying to establish a piece of good behaviour as a norm, the teacher should try to 'catch' every occurrence of it and make sure a reward is given. Once the behaviour is established, occasional rewards will suffice to maintain it. In the classroom, of course, it is not necessary to wait for a desired behaviour to occur in order to reward it; by explaining what is required to pupils (again the cognitive influence), so that they know what is going to earn the reward, the whole process of establishing the behaviour can be speeded up.

Another aspect of the frequency of reward concerns the optimum ratio of rewards to punishments. Some behaviourist writers on control have gone so far as to try to put a numerical value on this: a ratio of at least 4:1 in favour of rewards has been suggested. In the real classroom, there is no practicable way of counting the ratio of positive to negative experiences each pupil has; nevertheless, the notion that, for each pupil, rewards, in all the forms they can take, should clearly outweigh punishments or negative experiences is a sound one. Think of a very well-behaved pupil and consider what happens to him in the course of a school day (for example, getting his work satisfactorily done and appropriately marked by the teacher; being praised; receiving smiles; actually enjoying some of his work; finishing quickly and being allowed a free choice of activity). Compare this to what happens to a badly behaved one (for example, not getting through his work, being reprimanded, receiving frowns, hating his work, not finishing and therefore getting no free time). Then consider how each is probably treated when they go home. Is it fanciful to suggest that the preponderance of rewards received by the well-behaved one might well be, to some extent, a cause of his continuing good behaviour? If teachers could manage to make the classroom life of the badly behaved pupil more rewarding, then improvements in his behaviour could surely be expected.

4. The pupils' point of view

Insights into what types of reward are appropriate can be gleaned from trying to see classroom situations from the point of

view of the pupil, and considering his motives and his perceptions of the reasons for his behaviour. For instance, if it seems
that a pupil's misbehaviour is largely attention-seeking, then
attention from the teacher is obviously a potent reward. What
the teacher must do, therefore, is to try to supply such attention
as a reward for this pupil when he behaves well, while minimising, as far as is practicable, attention to his misbehaviour. The
general rule here is to try to give pupils reasons, from their point
of view, to behave well.

Another instance where trying to understand pupils' reasons for
behaving as they do can help in deciding upon an appropriate
reward is where a pupil's unwillingness to work stems from his
expectation of, and desire to avoid, failure. If this is his reason,
then clearly an effective reward for him when he does engage in
some work is success, and if his work can be structured, for
example, broken down into steps with which he can cope, so
that he actually does feel he is succeeding, then benefits should
result for both pupil and teacher.

Another result of trying to see things from the pupil's point of
view should be an increased awareness in the teacher that what
seems a reward to her may very well not seem so to a pupil. For
instance, it cannot be assumed, especially for secondary and
older primary pupils, that teacher approval, openly displayed,
will function as a reward. Frequently with pupils of this age
group there is a tendency for teacher approval for a pupil to
provoke peer group disapproval. When the latter is strong,
praise the teacher regards as a reward can have quite the opposite effect. It is not too difficult, by observing pupils' interactions, to see when teacher approval is likely to have this effect,
and other rewards should be used (although quieter, less public
praise might still be welcome).

Sometimes teachers hearing or reading about the behavioural
approach come to the conclusion, largely from the impersonal
and rather manipulative nature of many versions of this approach, that it is preferable that pupils do not know 'what the

teacher is up to,' in the sense of what behaviour is being rewarded by which rewards. When the behavioural approach is softened by cognitive insights, however, quite the opposite view should be taken, that is, that the more pupils know and understand what is going on, the better the likely effects on behaviour will be, as an incentive effect, as well as a reinforcement one, will be produced. In fact, one of the best ways to find effective rewards is to ask pupils, perhaps presenting a list from which to choose, which rewards they prefer, and to make it absolutely clear how they can earn these rewards.

As stated earlier, one of the rewards that many teachers are happy to use is social approval, in the form of praise from themselves. As a reward, notwithstanding the reservation that it can be negated by peer disapproval, this has much to recommend it. It helps, indeed requires, the teacher to try to be positive and pleasant to and about pupils, and it is extremely convenient to use. For it to be effective, however, it requires a genuine positive relationship between teacher and pupil. Mechanical, calculated smiles and praise, as well as being morally repellent, are very unlikely to be effective as a reward. Unless the relationship aspect of the BRR approach is sound, this frequently used, highly convenient, potentially powerful reward will be of little use.

5. Enhancing self-concepts

When selecting rewards to use, the teacher should pay attention to the desirability of improving pupils' self-concepts, especially the academic aspect of the self-concept. For the pupil with a poor academic self-concept, the reward most likely to enhance this is experience of success with work, which the teacher can attempt to arrange in the ways already mentioned. Here it is not so much misbehaviour that is the target, but the reasons or motives for misbehaviour. Before a pupil can experience success with work, however, he obviously has to engage in it in the first instance, and the teacher, in my view, should use any form of reward, however low, that is necessary to achieve this initial step. As far as a pupil's general self-concept is concerned, the social approval of the

'Mechanical, calculated smiles and praise . . . are very unlikely to be effective as a reward.'

teacher and other pupils, in the form of acceptance as a worthwhile member of the class, can be an enhancing influence. However, if misbehaviour is rewarded by his peers, then of course, while this may make him feel better about himself as a group member, it will serve to encourage his misbehaviour.

6. Inappropriate use of rewards

While the use of appropriate rewards is the main single strategy in the BRR approach, it is necessary to emphasise that reward is not always the most effective technique to use. Punishment has a place, as will be outlined later, but in addition, it is often more productive to change a situation that is causing misbehaviour than to try to deal with the misbehaviour by some reward or punishment strategy. For instance, if your pupils find it very difficult to work in fairly large co-operative groups making models, then rather than setting up some kind of reward system to establish good behaviour in this situation, it is probably more sensible and more effective to get them to work in smaller groups, or to set individual tasks for those pupils having most difficulty co-operating. Many of the organisational strategies mentioned in chapter 3 can be employed to make misbehaviour less likely, for example, changing seating arrangements to make them appropriate for different tasks. (It is very difficult, for instance, for pupils to work individually and silently when tightly packed round a table with the rest of a group.)

The use of punishment

If the above guidelines are followed, the use of rewards should be an effective means of changing behaviour. However, in my view rewards by themselves will not be sufficient as a classroom technique—there will also be a role for punishment, albeit a much smaller one than that for rewards. A fairly brief account of how punishments should be used now follows.

Punishment is rather a grim word. It is probably most often encountered in the terms corporal and capital punishment, and it has associations of guilt, blame and retribution. However, in recommending it as part of the BRR approach, I certainly do not mean to advocate extreme or cruel treatment of pupils, nor do I see its purposes as including retribution. In the classroom, punishment, in the sense I wish to use the term, occurs when a teacher deliberately takes action to ensure that the consequences of misbehaviour are unpleasant or undesired ones for the mis-behaving pupil. Punishment can take two forms: first, the application of something unpleasant (e.g. a reprimand) after an

undesired behaviour; and, second, the removal, after such behaviour, of something desired or pleasant (e.g. being separated
from a friend). Punishment in the classroom is intended simply
to lessen the likelihood of the recurrence of the undesired behaviour, and probably usually does this, although there is com-
paratively little hard evidence about its effects. Certainly most
teachers and parents seem to have faith in its effectiveness, since
they have kept on using it over the years, despite the many
objections made to it, on both ethical and practical grounds.
These ethical objections are considered later, together with those
against rewards. As far as practical objections are concerned, the
main ones made usually run along the following lines:

(1) Punishment is solely negative; it merely tells pupils what not
    to do.

(2) Punishment does not eliminate misbehaviour, but merely
    suppresses it temporarily.

(3) Punishment can cause fear and anxiety.

(4) Punishment can cause anger and resentment, leading to fur-
    ther misbehaviour.

There is something in each of these points, but they can be
countered. With regard to point (1), it surely cannot be disputed
that sometimes pupils need to be told what not to do, and if
punishment is used in conjunction with explanation, guidance
and reward then its negativity is well compensated for. When
misbehaviour is, say, dangerous, a quick, negative message is
essential to try to stop it. There is no time available for rewards
for incompatible behaviour to be effective. Point (2) probably
has some truth in it, but in the classroom it is often the case that
temporary suppression of behaviour is what is required. For
example, a teacher doesn't want pupils to forget how to chat to
friends in the classroom, simply to stop doing it for a while and
do it less often in future. Points (3) and (4), relating to fear,
anxiety and resentment, are much less likely to apply if punishments are fair, reasonable and moderate and explained and justified to pupils.

Various guidelines on the use of punishment in the classroom have been proposed. The following are appropriate for the BRR approach:

(1) Punishment is appropriate when a quick effect on mis-behaviour is necessary, that is when it is extreme and/or persistent and disruptive.

(2) A pupil should know exactly what he is being punished for. If he doesn't, then obviously he will be less able to decide to change the behaviour involved. Quite often teachers, because of their annoyance, fail to make clear exactly what the pupil's offence was.

(3) Punishment should be justified (i.e. a rule should clearly have been broken); consistent (i.e. the same punishment for the same offence, whoever commits it); and reasonable (i.e. its severity should be appropriate to the seriousness of the offence). If these rules are followed, pupils are more likely to accept a punishment as fair. If they are not followed, resentment (and perhaps refusal to accept the punishment) are likely to occur.

(4) Punishment should, ideally, immediately follow the onset of the behaviour which occasions it. If it has to be delayed the pupil should be clearly reminded why he is being punished. Quite often, especially in schools with formal detention systems, pupils can find themselves in detention several days after their offence was committed, having forgotten its exact nature.

(5) Trivial punishments should be avoided, as this may lead to pupils simply becoming accustomed to them and accepting them as routine parts of school life rather than something significant. For instance, an occasional firm reprimand is much more likely to be effective than the continual nagging of pupils.

(6) Any punishment which is likely to cause a high degree of fear or anxiety should be avoided. As well as being inhumane, such punishments are likely to be ineffective in

changing behaviour, as pupils in a state of high anxiety or fear are less likely to be able to make a clear link between their misbehaviour and punishment and to think rationally about whether and how to change their behaviour.

(7) As with rewards, what the teacher considers a punishment may not be seen as such by a pupil. It is therefore necessary for a teacher to try to put herself in the pupil's position when deciding on an appropriate punishment for an offence. For example, in the days of corporal punishment, it was not unusual for pupils to keep league tables of the number of times different members of the class received the cane or belt. Some pupils therefore deliberately tried to incur punishment to gain status in the eyes of their friends. In this way, what was regarded by teachers as the ultimate deterrent functioned for some pupils as a reward rather than a punishment. Similarly, teachers have to consider very carefully whether such 'punishments' as sitting with the girls, being kept in at break, etc., actually are punishments from the point of view of those receiving them.

(8) Punishments should not be issued in anger. If you are angry, you are less likely to be fair, reasonable and consistent.

'. . . teachers have to consider very carefully whether such "punishments" as sitting with the girls . . . actually are punishments from the point of view of those receiving them.'

You are also less likely to be willing and able to explain clearly to the pupil involved the nature of the offence and the justification for the punishment. There is a danger that you will be perceived by the pupil as issuing the punishment out of a desire for retribution, rather than to improve his behaviour (and there may well be some truth in this).

(9) Care should be taken to make it clear when giving a punishment that it is the behaviour, not the pupil, that is unacceptable. The message conveyed should be not, 'You are a bad person,' but, 'You are a good person who has done a bad thing'. Such a message is far less damaging to the pupil's self-concept, and much more constructive, in that it is obviously easier for the pupil to change an aspect of his behaviour than his moral character. A teacher who is angry is, of course, less likely to want, or to be able to, genuinely convey such a message, and this is another reason not to issue punishments in anger. Disappointment that the pupil has let himself down is a far better feeling to express if a punishment has to be given.

(10) As far as is possible, punishments should encourage pupils to behave better, as well as discourage them from behaving badly. In other words there should ideally be an element of incentive included in them. For instance, rather than separating a misbehaving pupil from his friends for ever, or for a year or a term or a week, it is more effective to separate him for, say, 15 minutes and tell him that, if he behaves well for this time, he will be allowed to rejoin his friends. This tactic is far more likely to produce an improvement in behaviour, and less resentment, than a longer sentence. If it does not, a longer ban can still be given, and will probably be seen as more reasonable by the pupil.

Although punishment is normally considered a behavioural technique, the guidelines above (especially (2), (3), (4), (6), (7), (8) and (9)) are heavily influenced by the cognitive element of the BRR approach. How the pupil interprets what is happening, and how well he understands the reasons for his punishment are important determinants of the success or failure of this technique. Also, the quality of the relationship between teacher and pupil is important in determining the effectiveness of reprimands and punishments in general. A serious 'telling-off' by a teacher who is liked and respected by a pupil (who believes the teacher genuinely likes him) is quite a different matter from one by a teacher who is not so highly regarded.

In schools there is a wide range of punishments available. These include reprimands, withdrawal of privileges (assuming pupils have some), written punishment exercises, and formal and informal detention. 'Logical consequences' are often a very effective form of classroom punishment, partly because they are usually accepted as fair by pupils. Into this category come such punishments as tidying the classroom for making a mess or staying in at break to finish work which should have been done earlier. As stated earlier, being separated (temporarily) from friends or being (again temporarily) denied an enjoyable (or at least preferred) activity can be very effective ways of motivating pupils to behave better in order to achieve restoration of privileges. Punishments with an element of humour (though not involving the humiliation of pupils) can be effective, in that they help to maintain an atmosphere of friendliness between teacher and pupils. For instance, I once knew a teacher who kept football supporters' scarves of the local teams as blackboard dusters. For a serious offence, the miscreant was required to clear the board with his favourite team's scarf. While pupils certainly didn't like doing this (and it was therefore an effective punishment) the whole business was also good fun for all concerned, and it was a happy, though tightly run, classroom thanks to this teacher's combination of firmness and good nature.

A particularly useful punishment, especially for secondary schools, is instant, temporary exclusion from class. This has an immediacy which few other punishments have. It allows the teacher to demonstrate that she is in charge, it removes a disruptive pupil from the scene of the disruption, thus normally ending it, and it allows both a chance to cool off. Sometimes it is used by teachers on an individual basis with the pupil merely being told to wait outside the classroom for a time. This can be ineffective, however, as a pupil may not take it seriously, perhaps making faces through the window in the door if one is present. And what happens if a friend decides to misbehave in order to join the excluded one? What is much better is for the school to set up a system for such exclusion.

Various such arrangements, known as sin-bins or time-out facilities, have been tried out. Some years ago in a newspaper article I suggested a version in which in a secondary school (or a large primary school), a pupil who committed a seriously disruptive offence would be sent by the teacher to a special workplace within the school, supervised, ideally, by a senior member of staff engaged in marking or office work. The pupil's name would be recorded and he would be given prepared written work to do, simple enough for no help to be required. At the end of the period the pupil would rejoin his class for the next lesson, and the teacher who had sent him would, as soon as practicable, send a brief statement of the nature of the offence to be added to the record. While no recriminations or investigations would take place at this point, any pupil who was excluded (say) three times in one month would be the subject of an enquiry into his behaviour involving his parents and further action considered, including possible suspension.

Perhaps the most obvious strength of such a punishment is, as stated above, its immediacy—at the time when I first suggested this version teachers were understandably bemoaning the fact that with the demise of corporal punishment they could not do something 'here and now' to reassert their authority when it was seriously challenged. But equally useful is the fact that it involves senior staff in monitoring behaviour throughout the school. This gets the message across to pupils that serious misbehaviour in a classroom is not a trivial matter involving only them and the teacher concerned, but something that concerns the school at the highest level. It also means that patterns of misbehaviour can be identified and particular pupils and teachers advised appropriately. In a smaller school the same basic procedure could be followed in a less formal way, so long as someone was available to keep an eye on the occasional excluded pupil.

All punishments used in the classroom must be in line with school policy, and if you are in any doubt about a punishment you must consult senior staff. Just as with rules, you may need support with regard to punishment. Secondary schools often have special arrangements for persistent offenders, including such things as cards on which teachers make a note of misbehaviour, and punishment used within the classroom must be compatible with such systems.

The nature and use of rewards and punishments has now been dealt with in some detail. In the next chapter, some real-life examples of how they can be put into practice in the classroom are given. Before that, however, there are two more strategies, relevant to both rewards and punishment, which merit brief treatment. These are modelling and extinction. Modelling is the term commonly used for the way in which people's behaviour and attitudes tend to be adopted by others around them. In classrooms, there is considerable scope for this sort of effect, with both teacher and pupils likely to be models for others. Investigations into what makes modelling more likely to occur have produced various lists of factors. The following seem relevant to the classroom.

Imitative behaviour is more likely to occur if:

(1) The model is warm and caring.
(2) The model has power to control and dispense rewards and punishments.
(3) Imitative behaviour is rewarded.
(4) The model is rewarded.
(5) The model has high status.
(6) There are several models behaving in the same way.

and less likely to occur if

(7) The model is punished.

Some writers on class control suggest that teachers should deliberately set up situations in which imitation of desired behaviour is likely, that is, that modelling should consciously be used as a technique for changing behaviour. Without going this far, but simply regarding modelling as a phenomenon that is likely to occur in the classroom, it is interesting to note that, in the main, the effect of modelling should be to increase the effectiveness of the judicious use of rewards and punishments. When a pupil is rewarded for good behaviour, he is more likely to be taken as a model. When imitative good behaviour is rewarded, it is more likely to recur. The greater the number of pupils engaged in good behaviour, the more likely it is to be imitated by others. Punished behaviour is less likely to be imitated. Also, points (1), (2) and (5) in the above list should apply to a teacher taking a BRR approach and make her attitudes more likely to be adopted. There is a less welcome implication from the list, of course. This is that misbehaviour by high-status peer group members, especially if rewarded by attention and approval from other children, is also likely to be imitated. This is a danger to be guarded against, by trying to make sure such pupils misbehave as little as possible, through the use of rewards and punishments.

Extinction, as previously explained, is the term used for the well-established behavioural principle that behaviour which is not rewarded will normally occur less and less frequently and finally disappear. On this basis, teachers are frequently recommended to ignore misbehaviour, in the expectation that, without the reward of teacher attention, it will vanish. However, in my view, extinction is not very often to be recommended in the classroom as a means of changing behaviour, for three main reasons. First, teachers cannot afford to ignore bad behaviour which disrupts pupils' learning. Such behaviour has to be stopped. Second, even if the teacher is able to withhold her attention, other pupils' attention and approval is likely to act as a reward, perpetuating the misbehaviour. Third, misbehaviour is often intrinsically rewarding to the offender. Even though the teacher and other pupils pay little or no attention to it, such behaviour will persist. It is only with very trivial misbehaviour that none of these points will apply and that ignoring by the teacher is likely to lead to genuine extinction.

To conclude this account of how the BRR approach can be put into practice, it is necessary to examine some of the ethical and practical criticisms that might be made of it. The strong cognitive element within it should excuse it from the charge that is often made against a purely behavioural approach—that is, that such an approach fails to do justice to the importance of pupils' thoughts, perceptions, feelings and relationships and is therefore limited, cold and mechanical.

Thoughts, feelings, perceptions and relationships are important elements in the BRR approach. However, like the behavioural approach, the BRR one involves the teacher in laying down rules and using rewards and punishments in getting pupils to behave in accordance with them. The teacher's right to do this is often questioned. Why should pupils, who are often in school wholly or partly against their will, be made to behave in ways they don't want? In my view, the answer to this question lies in the nature of the role teachers are given, paid for and expected to fill by society. Teachers are given many responsibilities, of which two main ones are to ensure that their pupils come to no physical harm and to promote their learning. This means that teacher and pupil are not equals, and that along with the teacher's responsibilities must go certain powers, including the right to require pupils not to behave in ways which might endanger their own or other pupils' safety and learning.

More particular objections to the use of reward and punishment are to regard reward as bribery and punishment as inhumane. The term 'bribery' is normally used to apply to the giving of money or some other reward as payment for doing something morally objectionable. For instance, if I offer a policeman money in return for his falling to arrest me for some crime, this is clearly bribery, but if I offer a painter money to paint my window-frames, it is not. In the classroom pupils are given rewards, not for behaviour which is in the teacher's interest only, but which is in their own best interests. Surely only if the teacher does not genuinely believe that it will be good for a pupil to behave in the way for which he is being rewarded can she be guilty of bribery. Any teacher who still feels guilty about using rewards should consider for a moment the everyday experiences of the many fortunate pupils who come from happy homes with caring parents, who get on well with their teachers and schoolmates, and who try hard at school and do well. Every day such a pupil's life is filled with rewards, such as kindness, approval, praise, success, satisfaction from his work, presents for exam success, and so on. Reward is a continual, natural experience for him. Teachers who use rewards to improve the behaviour of less fortunate pupils are simply going a little way towards redressing an imbalance.

With regard to punishment, it is certainly difficult to dispute that in some forms it is cruel and ethically unacceptable. But the kinds of punishment recommended in this chapter, for example, reprimands, temporary separation from friends and staying in at breaks, have little in common with corporal punishment or other extreme forms (it is, in fact, unfortunate that the same word has to be used) and are surely not inhumane. Ultimately, each teacher has to make up her own mind about ethical questions, of course, but my view is strongly that rules, rewards and punishments are necessary and morally justified in the classroom and, indeed, that a teacher who could achieve order by using them, but is unwilling to do so (and cannot achieve it by other means) is acting irresponsibly and unprofessionally.

As well as these ethical objections, practical criticisms of the approach recommended can be made. First, what if support from senior staff is not forthcoming when needed, for instance, when rules are broken and punishments refused? Assuming that the teacher has made sure that her rules, punishments, and, indeed, rewards, are in line with school policy, I believe she is entitled to such support and will receive it, so long as she is seen to be making a genuine effort to deal with her problems and is not constantly expecting senior staff to sort things out for her. In many schools, without such occasional support, I honestly do not believe that the BRR (or any) approach to control can be really successful, for it is vitally important, especially in the early days with a difficult class, to make sure that punishments 'stick'. A punishment successfully avoided constitutes, in effect, a reward for misbehaviour. Where a pupil resists the attempts of senior staff to enforce a legitimate punishment, the school has to be prepared to suspend him until he and his parents agree that he will conform to basic school rules.

Another practical difficulty in applying any approach to control is that not all teachers in the school will take the same line with pupils. For example, some will reject the use of rewards, and some will have rules which are more lax than others. In the primary school this will have a less marked effect than in the secondary school, as each primary teacher has her own class most of the day. However, ideally, in both kinds of school, the same kind of approach would be employed by all teachers. This is unlikely ever to happen, of course, especially in secondary schools, and the effect of pupils being subjected to different types of regime will be that it will take them longer to learn which kinds of behaviour are acceptable and unacceptable, and will increase the need for patience and perseverance on the teacher's part.

In the next chapter, I shall outline some examples of the BRR approach in action.

The main points of this chapter

● Applying the BRR approach with a new class or classes, the teacher should initially be firm and pleasant, introduce rules, be prepared to use punishments and set straightforward work.

- Gradually, rewards aimed at particular problems or general behaviour should be introduced to encourage good behaviour and a progressive attempt should be made to raise the level of rewards in terms of educational desirability.

- Rewards ranging widely from more to less educationally desirable are available in the classroom, viz. reward intrinsic to learning activities, success experience, praise and approval, preferred activities, token and tangible rewards.

- Rewards at a lower than necessary level may have the effect of undermining or weakening the intrinsic reward of an activity.

- To minimise this effect, it should be stressed to pupils that lower level rewards are symbols of having done well rather than payment for it.

- The level of reward effective with a pupil or class can be raised by associating higher level rewards with lower level ones which are proving effective.

- In the early stages of establishing a behaviour, reward should be frequent; once the behaviour is established occasional reward should be sufficient to maintain it.

- The choice of an appropriate reward can be aided by considering how the pupil or pupils involved will see the situation and possible rewards.

- Rewards likely to enhance pupils' self-concepts are desirable.

- Rather than use a reward to change behaviour, it is often more effective to change the situation which has acted as a stimulus for the behaviour.

- Punishment in the classroom can be the application of something unpleasant or the removal of something pleasant and is intended to lessen the likelihood of the recurrence of behaviour.

- Various practical objections to the use of punishment in the classroom can be made, but can be countered.

- A set of guidelines for the use of punishment can be constructed which takes into account how pupils interpret situations, the importance of their understanding of the reasons for their punishment and the quality of their relationship with the teacher.

- Various punishments are available in schools; a 'sin-bin' facility is a very useful addition to the usual set, because of its immediacy.

- Modelling (the imitation of the behaviour of others) will occur in classrooms and can enhance the effects of the judicious use of rewards and punishments.

- Extinction is not of much use in the classroom, as much misbehaviour needs to be stopped quickly, other pupils reward misbehaviour by their attention and misbehaviour is often intrinsically rewarding to the offender.

- Ethical objections can be made to the BRR approach, for example: Have teachers the right to make pupils behave in ways they do not want to? Is reward bribery? Is punishment cruel? These can be countered, but each teacher has to judge their validity in terms of her own values.

- A teacher employing the BRR approach will experience difficulties if support is not available from senior staff when required, and it will take pupils longer to learn acceptable ways of behaving if other teachers take a different approach with a class.

Discussion questions

1. Do you agree with the idea of 'catch them being good'? Do you think you would find it difficult to reward the occasional good behaviour of a generally badly behaved pupil? If so, why?

2. Which of the six categories of reward would you use in the classroom? If there are some you would reject, why?

3. Which kinds of punishment, if any, do you think are appropriate for the age-range you teach?

4. Do you think teachers have a moral right to use (i) reward and (ii) punishment?

6

THE BRR APPROACH
IN ACTION: SOME
EXAMPLES

In this chapter I shall present five real-life 'case studies', that is, examples of attempts to deal with control problems involving the application of some of the cognitive and behavioural principles comprising the BRR approach described in the last chapter. The first of these is a strategy I myself put into practice some years ago with a secondary school third-year class. The second was more recently carried out with a first-year secondary class by a student on placement, and the third and fourth are primary school examples where I acted as a consultant to the teachers concerned. The last is another personal experience. These examples are intended to be illustrative rather than prescriptive, but the strategies described might well be applicable to other settings.

1. Settling a difficult class

Some years ago, as a secondary English teacher, I experienced considerable difficulty with a third-year bottom set for English, a 'boys only' class. This was not, incidentally, the same class as that mentioned in chapter 2 (the George Best story), but a class which I later discovered to be a much more pleasant and likeable one, if not particularly work-oriented. I was fairly experienced by this time and was somewhat surprised by the difficulty I was finding in getting these boys to settle down to their work when they arrived for their English lessons each day, especially on Wednesdays at 10.00 am, when they would arrive, not as a class, but in groups of four or five over a period of five minutes or so, with some quite late. There was general red-faced hilarity and excited, muffled discussions, presumably of what they had just been doing. When all had finally gathered and I tried to start the lesson, the difficulties continued. During the lessons they were inattentive and fidgety and did not settle down well to anything they were left to do by themselves.

My first, fairly automatic response to this behaviour, which was similar, if less extreme, on three of the other occasions I saw them in the week, was to remonstrate with them, calmly and politely at first, but decreasingly so, as I became annoyed when their misbehaviour continued. My reprimands became sharper, and the atmosphere in the classroom became unpleasant and strained as the boys grew resentful. In addition, a considerable amount of time was being wasted at the beginnings of lessons in waiting for them to arrive and settle, and the work I had prepared for them, which I was fairly confident was potentially interesting and worthwhile, was not getting a fair chance to be so found by them.

After a few weeks—perhaps rather late—I started to make serious enquiries as to why they had been arriving late and in such an excited state. The boys were reluctant to say much, of course, but I gathered that, at least on Wednesdays, their disarray and merriment had more to do with events in their previous class, a music lesson, than with misbehaviour en route. From further enquiry with colleagues (and picking up odd bits of information from the boys), I was able to piece together the whole picture. Their new music teacher was a young man, who (despite considerable efforts by senior staff to help him) was to decide, fairly shortly afterwards, upon a different career. Music teachers in secondary schools have a difficult job at the best of times, with large numbers of pupils to deal with, many of whom do not regard music as a serious subject. The new teacher augmented these normal difficulties with a 'mad professor' appearance and eccentric behaviour, including the habit of becoming totally engrossed in his piano playing, with his back to a misbehaving class, then suddenly whipping round and, on at least two occasions, literally falling off his stool. Predictably, with a third-year bottom set, horseplay swiftly became the norm among the pupils, and the lessons became chaotic, unintentional entertainments. Seeing things from the pupils' point of view, it was not surprising that they arrived in the manner and mood that they did for the next lesson. I also discovered that the teacher who preceded me on another day, while not up to the same comic standard, also tended to let the boys become more than a bit over-excited.

After this 'cognitive' exercise of finding out what I could about the reasons for the boys' misbehaviour (not ones that I could do much about) and trying to see things from their point of view, which much reduced my annoyance at them, I decided to employ some behavioural tactics. Firstly, I would try to establish behaviour incompatible with arriving late and failing to settle, and, secondly, I would do so positively, by rewarding the desired behaviour, although it would obviously be difficult to find something more attractive than hanging about in the corridors and stairways, gleefully going over the fun of the previous lesson.

The strategy I employed was as follows. For each of the first four days of the week, the boys were given ten words which they were to learn for a spelling test next day. The words were copied from the blackboard at the end of each lesson into a special small notebook. I deliberately chose the words to be on the easy side, so that, even without much serious study at home (homework was not their strong point), most of the boys would get most of the words correct. Each day (Monday to Thursday) when the class arrived for their English lesson, they were given a test. A slip of paper was ready at every place, I had pencils ready to lend if needed, and I started as soon as the bulk of the class arrived. Stragglers had to begin at the point we had reached and therefore missed the chance to get the first few words correct. I

'Their new music teacher was a young man, who . . . was to decide, fairly shortly afterwards, upon a different career.'

had explained this in advance, openly saying that part of the purpose of the spelling test was to get them to arrive promptly. The class was divided into spelling groups of four members each, chosen by me so that the teams were of roughly equal spelling ability and motivation to one another. Each group with an overall weekly success rate of 70% or better was given 15 minutes free time during the Friday afternoon English lesson, when any quiet activity was allowed. I used the last ten minutes or so of each lesson to mark the test done at the beginning, while the boys worked on the follow-up to the main part of the lesson.

A spin-off benefit was that I could obtain peace and quiet while they worked by presenting a pained expression to any disruption and saying: 'If you don't *want* your marks . . .'. This almost invariably had the desired effect. They were keen to get their marks and make a note of them.

Unlike a thoroughgoing behaviourist, I made no attempt to measure the improvement in the boys' behaviour objectively. What mattered to me was my subjective judgment. In fact, I was delighted by the improvement in behaviour. The class seemed to take a genuine liking to the new arrangement, after being reassured that the marks did not 'count' for reports, etc. They started arriving on time, with some actually running to get to the room early. They quickly settled to the test, and, after it, continued to behave in a largely peaceful fashion. Any stragglers received strong disapproval from their team-mates for losing points by missing the early words, and after a few days almost no-one was late. All were keen to know their marks, which they solemnly recorded in their notebooks at the end of the lesson.

Each Friday, thanks to my careful selection of words and group members, most of the groups qualified for free time. However, while pleased with this reward, they were equally interested in the relative performances of the teams, and, at their request, I kept running totals week by week. I was a little surprised that this competition, which I had not really planned (since I expected most groups to be successful most of the time), was taken so seriously. However, upon reflection, it is, perhaps, not so surprising, given the liking that even adults have for TV quiz shows, 'Trivial Pursuits', and so on. The fun of competition was a reward I had not really taken into account. Another product of the strategy that I had not anticipated was its effect on the academic self-concepts of the boys. This was a group grown accustomed to failure and to regarding themselves as no good at school work. For once, perhaps for the first time for years for some, they were engaging in work where they were actually achieving success, and had objective evidence for this, in the marks and free time that they were earning. Thinking back, although I had not consciously planned this boost to the self-esteem of the pupils, it seems fairly obvious that it had an important role in making the strategy so effective. In fact, things worked out so well that, after a few weeks, I was able to drop the free time as a reward, replacing it with a suitably light Friday afternoon whole-class lesson. The spelling lists, tests and marks, however, I kept going for the rest of the year, latterly reducing them to two lists of fifteen words per week. As well as a great improvement in behaviour, there was, perhaps even more importantly, a marked change in atmosphere in the classroom. For at least part of the time (not all of their work was as eagerly attempted as the spelling), the boys were trying hard and enjoying the experience. I was able to change from a mood of annoyance and the issuing of reprimands, to genuine pleasantness and approval for effort and achievement.

Two connected objections to this strategy have been raised by people to whom I have described it: first, whether the spelling activity was educationally worthwhile; and, second, if it was not, how could the time spent upon it be justified? In answer to the first, I believe that the spelling at worst did no harm, although its purpose certainly was to improve behaviour rather than spelling. At least, the boys had some practice with common words and accepted that it was a good thing to get them correct. Doing spelling in this way did not prevent me from also carrying out the probably more profitable strategy of attending to their spelling of words in their own writing. The boost to their morale of getting lots of words correct and earning a reward was certainly educationally worthwhile, as was the general improvement in relations with me. With regard to the time taken up by the spelling, it has to be remembered that, previous to my introducing it, time was being wasted with late arrivals and recriminations. I feel sure that, even if the spelling cannot be justified educationally, the time 'wasted' on it was certainly no more than the time previously wasted by the misbehaviour. Overall, therefore, I believe this strategy was a very worthwhile one, and I would recommend it in situations where a class is having serious difficulties in arriving and settling to work; with primary pupils, it would, I think, be necessary to stress that it was basically a game, as they might take it just too seriously. Even some of the fourteen-year-olds described here became quite heated when they felt their team-mates had let them down, and I had occasionally to exact promises that no-one would be 'sorted-out' later. Spelling, as such, is not an essential ingredient of the strategy. Basic factual knowledge in any subject-area could serve as the content of the tests.

To conclude this account, it is perhaps worthwhile repeating that as well as the reward of free time upon which the strategy was built, various other rewards came into play, not all of which I was conscious of until later. These were peer approval, teacher approval (added to that of peers) and success experience. Punishment also figured, with stragglers punished by lower marks and peer disapproval, and misbehaviour at the end of the lesson was punished by the threat of not getting marks back. Only once, as I remember, was it necessary actually to withhold them, which again is evidence of how seriously the boys took the whole business.

2. Ten green bottles

What follows is an account of a strategy employed with a first-year mixed-ability secondary class. The teacher who carried it out was actually a student on a short (five-week) placement in the school who was given responsibility for the class for two lessons per week after the first week. What she did was based loosely upon an intervention (as it was called) described in an American case study discussed in College shortly before she went out to school.

The problem, as she saw it, was the generally over-excited and noisy behaviour of many members of this first-year class. In particular, two aspects of this misbehaviour troubled her. These were, first, their tendency to shout out answers to her questions, rather than put their hands up and wait, as requested; and, second, their habit of leaving their seats at odd times without particular need and without her permission. The teacher felt they were rather immature as a group and untrained in what she regarded as the proper ways to behave in a classroom. Upon enquiry, she discovered that many of them had come from a primary school regarded by most teachers in the secondary school as too permissive in its attitude to behaviour. None of the children, she believed, were being insolent or deliberately disruptive. On the contrary, she found them keen to please and to contribute to lessons, hence the shouting-out she found so annoying.

Her first step in trying to deal with the problem was to make it clear to the class just what she expected, by introducing two simple rules about shouting-out and seat-leaving. This, together with reprimands for those who broke them, worked to some extent, but the need for reprimands was frequent, resulting in many interruptions to work. In addition, some pupils reacted to them in a hurt and sometimes resentful fashion, and she found herself getting annoyed. She feared that the positive relationship she had quickly formed with the class was in danger. Her task, as she now saw it, was to find a way to get the class to behave better, in particular to observe the two rules, without recourse to frequent reprimands with their unwelcome consequences.

The strategy she employed, an adaptation of the one we had discussed, involved a combination of reward and punishment. She had noted early in her contact with the pupils how they had enjoyed a boys versus girls quiz held by their usual teacher on a topic they had covered, and decided to use this kind of activity as a reward. A few minutes at the end of each lesson, with relatively easy questions from a children's quiz book (answered on a 'first hand up' basis), would be devoted to the quiz, with cumulative scores being kept from day to day. However, quiz time had to be earned, and this is where the punishment aspect of the strategy figured. At the beginning of each lesson, she drew the outlines of 'ten green bottles' on the top of the blackboard. It was explained to the class, on the first occasion, that if the ten green bottles were still firmly 'standing on the wall' at the end of the lesson, they would have five minutes of a boys versus girls quiz. However, each time someone broke the hands or seats rule, one green bottle would be removed and with it one half-minute of quiz time. The pupils thought this was an excellent idea, and there were some ingenious suggestions as to how, if, say, a boy were responsible for the loss of a bottle, the boys might get fewer opportunities to answer questions. After some discussion, during which the teacher felt pleased that the children were beginning to become very involved in the scheme, it was decided that this would be too complicated, and the teacher's original plan was followed.

In the teacher's opinion, the strategy worked very well. Although she made no attempt to quantify misbehaviour before or after its introduction, she was sure that it greatly improved the pupils' behaviour. On the first few occasions several half-minutes were lost, but this reduced to a steady one or two per lesson. The quiz was being given three or four minutes per day, and with fairly easy questions and many hands being raised (which, incidentally, helped to establish the second rule), the scores soon mounted up, to the children's enjoyment.

The benefits were threefold. First, misbehaviour lessened; second, there were far fewer interruptions to lessons. Even when it was necessary to remove a bottle, the teacher merely made a rueful face, and, in mock tragic fashion, dramatically slashed through one of the bottles on the blackboard, without comment, other than 'oh dear'. The pupil who had occasioned the loss was usually crestfallen, and the rest of the class very censorious. The third benefit of the strategy, perhaps the most important one, was the improvement in classroom atmosphere and teacher–pupil relationships. From the unpleasantness of constant re-crimination, the teacher had moved to a means of control that she and the pupils actually found fun. She was able to be disappointed with them when quiz time was lost and happy when the full five minutes was earned. She now felt the pupils liked her and looked forward to coming to her lessons, and that she was more firmly in control.

This example shows, again, how reward and punishment can work in combination, and how punishment need not be grim and cruel but can be moderate and light-hearted, while still effective. It is hard to imagine any pupil being caused fear or anxiety by punishment like this. Furthermore, the teacher did not employ her rewards and punishments in a cold, mechanical way. There are cognitive influences in operation, such as her being able to see and take into consideration the fact that the pupils' misbehaviour was not intended to be disruptive or insolent, and that there was a need to avoid damage to their basically positive attitudes and eagerness to contribute. Her choice of reward also shows her willingness to take the pupils' view of classroom life into account. Making a mental note of what pupils seem to enjoy is an efficient way of building up a stock of potential rewards.

Overall, the teacher was very pleased, if slightly surprised, by the success of her strategy, and resolved to use it, or variants of it, in similar circumstances in future.

3. A fresh start

This third case study is a description of a global strategy, that is, one involving the whole daily management of the behaviour of a class. The teacher involved had just moved from a rural primary school, where she had taught seven- and eight-year-olds, to a large, urban council estate school, where she was given a larger class of ten- and eleven-year-old pupils. After a couple of weeks, she was dismayed by the change in her classroom life. In the rural school, she had taught a class of engaging, easily con-trolled children who clearly liked her and were generally keen to please. In addition, she had a very supportive, long-established headteacher who was held in great respect by her pupils. In this setting she did not see herself as having any control problems worthy of the name.

Her move occasioned a culture-shock for her. The new school, as well as being much larger, was overcrowded. In the open-plan layout, she and her class were allocated what seemed a very small area. She was very conscious of the behaviour of other teachers and their classes, and of the effects of misbehaviour on the part of her own children upon other classes. With a much larger staff, relationships between the head and class teachers, though good, were inevitably less close than those she had been used to, and she no longer had the security of knowing that help and support would be readily available if she required them. Her new pupils, or at least a large minority of them, were not automatically respectful towards her, and seemed relatively indifferent as to whether she liked them and approved of their behaviour. Much of what she had taken for granted in her old classroom no longer applied. The class failed (or refused, as she saw it) to fall silent when requested. Children interrupted when she was speaking to the whole class or to a group. Much minor misbehaviour seemed to take place all the time. Pupils wandered about the area for no good reason, interfered with others' work by talking to them or teasing them, chatted rather than worked, squabbled over borrowed or lost pencils and rubbers, shouted when only quiet talking was allowed, and so on. There was so much misbehaviour that the teacher found it difficult to identify particular incidents for attention.

To try to deal with all this, she employed the techniques which she had used rarely but successfully in her last school, namely reprimands, heart-to-heart talks, and occasional detentions at breaks. These met with only limited success. The class was not totally out of control; indeed, as far as she could see, some nearby classes were behaving even worse, but it was an unhappy, unproductive teaching situation. She felt she was acting as a policeman rather than a teacher, devoting most of her time and energy simply to control, constantly remonstrating and moralising with pupils about their behaviour. She did make a conscious effort to notice and praise good behaviour, but this seemed to have little effect upon the majority of pupils, who seldom engaged in it. She felt many of her pupils did not like her or want to please her, and, indeed, that to some extent their misbehaviour was directly intended to annoy and upset her.

After considerable reflection about this unfortunate situation, the teacher decided that what was needed was a fresh start with the class, with a quite different type of regime. Her new approach embodied the following changes.

(1) Accepting the children's present behaviour as being just how they had learned to behave in school, rather than as deliberately disruptive and intended to annoy or upset her.

(2) Accepting that, at present, neither her continual reprimands, nor her praise, carried much weight with the pupils.

(3) Attempting to focus on good behaviour rather than misbehaviour.

(4) Trying to find rewards that would be effective with the pupils.

(5) Devising a system that would allow these rewards to be used for all aspects of pupils' behaviour.

(6) Restricting reprimands and other punishments to extreme misbehaviour.

She decided against formally introducing a set of rules at this point, as she felt the pupils knew clearly how they were expected to behave, despite their misbehaviour. However, she did explain explicitly to the class what she was going to do and why, emphasising that she was sure they were as fed up as she was with all the rows that they were getting.

The new regime was as follows. First, the class was allowed to choose friendship groups for seating, or at least allowed a part in this process. To avoid the usual difficulties caused by pupils being rejected, each pupil was asked to record, secretly, the names of two others he would like in his group. From this information, the teacher was able to construct six groups of five pupils, including some mutually chosen pairs in each. Each group was asked to decide a name for itself and to construct a large wall-display card, ready to receive stars. The teacher explained that, instead of giving rows (except for very bad behaviour) she was going to try to ignore misbehaviour and instead give a star for any good behaviour she noticed, either by an individual, which would earn his group a star, or by a whole group, which would earn the group two stars. For every five stars, a gold star would be given, and for three gold stars, a special reward. The special reward, decided after class discussion, was to be an opportunity for the group to play one of a number of board games, in class time. This reward, of course, had to be 'cleared' by the headteacher.

The new regime started, with the teacher finding herself surprised, first, by how many instances of good behaviour were, in fact, to be found, and, second, by the reluctance she had to overcome to give stars for what she would have regarded, in her last school, as routine good behaviour. Her natural inclination was clearly to take good behaviour for granted and to watch out for misbehaviour. When she saw good behaviour, she told the class about it before awarding the star, e.g., 'John has gone right across the room to fetch a book without disturbing anyone', or, 'All the Munsters have handed in their maths open at the right place with all their corrections done'.

The system was a success. While behaviour did not become perfect, there was a marked improvement, and, perhaps even more importantly, the atmosphere in the area and teacher–pupil relationships improved greatly. From being a person who nagged and reprimanded the children, the teacher had become a person who noticed and rewarded good behaviour. She felt that the crucial factor in operation was neither the stars nor the games, but the social approval within the groups when members earned stars, and, indeed, the disapproval when they misbehaved, for she used the removal of a star as a punishment for serious misbehaviour, although this was not really in line with her original intention. Another strength of this system, she felt, was that even if a group fell well behind the others in the pursuit of stars, it still had the incentive of the next game to help it to keep trying.

This example shows how a whole-class reward system can be effective when normal tactics have been unsuccessful. The

teacher's breakthrough was to recognise that the pupils' misbehaviour, which she was taking almost as a personal attack, or
at least a challenge to her authority, was, more probably, simply
the result of their having learned a different set of norms for
classroom behaviour from those she had been used to in her last
school. This new awareness of the nature and reasons for the
pupils' misbehaviour led her to be able to accept how they were
behaving as a starting-point and to look for ways to improve
their behaviour. The ways she found, happily, involved acknowledging improvements in behaviour and being pleasant to the
children, rather than identifying misbehaviour and being unpleasant. This brought consequent benefits to teacher–pupil relationships. Another important factor in the success of the
strategy was the teacher's realisation that, with a class like this,
initially rather indifferent to her and her views, peer-group approval was likely to be a much more potent reward than teacher
praise. A third noteworthy feature of the strategy was the choice
of class time to play a chosen game as the special reward. As
well as the usefulness of this in motivating even groups who had
fallen behind, as mentioned earlier, it also, since it was clearly
enjoyed by the pupils, served to lessen any danger of the stars
being seen as 'baby-stuff' by the more sophisticated members of
the class.

4. Squared paper

This case-study is different from the others, in that it involves an
attempt to cope with the very difficult behaviour of one particular pupil in a primary class. Elizabeth arrived as a new nine-
year-old pupil in a small primary school. Her family, which had
recently undergone some significant changes, had moved from a
nearby town. Her mother, in initial discussions with the teacher
and headteacher, revealed that Elizabeth now had a step-father
and a new baby sister. A veil was drawn over the character and
whereabouts of her original father, but he was certainly not on
the scene. Her mother found Elizabeth very difficult at home;
she told lies and had stolen from her mother's handbag. In her

previous school, she had experienced many difficulties, being involved in much misbehaviour in the classroom and being bullied in the playground. Her mother hoped all would be well in the new school.

Unsurprisingly, all was not well. A similar pattern began to emerge. Elizabeth got on very badly with other members of the generally well-behaved class, who claimed, upon questioning, that they had tried to make her welcome, but that she spoiled playground games, hit them, and so on. Within a short time she seemed rejected by her new classmates in both classroom and playground. No-one wanted to sit with her or take part in any co-operative work with her. She sulked and had occasional tantrums in the classroom, told obvious lies and was very strongly suspected of pilfering from pupils and the teacher's stock of materials. Her relationship with the teacher was almost as bad as that with her fellow pupils. She seemed desperate for attention and continually pestered the teacher at inappropriate times about inappropriate matters. Even more infuriating was her inability or, in the teacher's opinion, refusal to get on with her work. Notwithstanding her reasonable ability, she would sit for long times doing nothing despite all the teacher's attempts at encouragement or recrimination. In addition to all this, she had a facial twitch and some other odd mannerisms.

It seemed clear that psychological help was necessary for Elizabeth, and the process of obtaining this was set in motion. In the meantime, the school had to do something to try to improve Elizabeth's behaviour, in the interests not only of herself, but of her classmates and teacher. Her mother was glad to join in further discussions about handling her in school. Any problems at home were to be left for the attention of the Psychological Service.

It was decided to try to break away from the tyranny of Elizabeth's misbehaviour and use a reward strategy to encourage good behaviour. As she always seemed very keen to have her mother's approval, the plan adopted was to utilise this as the ultimate reward by sending home only positive messages about Elizabeth's behaviour. This would earn her mother's praise, whereas previously communication with home had always been to pass on bad news about her behaviour. The strategy, in detail, was as follows. As Elizabeth's misbehaviour was so all-encompassing, it was decided to reward her for behaving acceptably for periods of time, rather than attempt to target specific desirable behaviour. Each Monday Elizabeth was given a sheet of paper divided into columns for the five days. Each column was sub-divided horizontally into five periods of time: before break, break, after break, lunch-time and afternoon, making a grid of 25 boxes. At the end of each of these periods, the teacher put a tick in the appropriate box if Elizabeth had behaved acceptably (playground and lunch-time supervisors were asked to report significant misbehaviour).

On Friday, if Elizabeth had twenty or more boxes ticked, she was given the sheet to take home to her mother with a comment at the bottom to the effect that her behaviour had been excellent; if she had fifteen or more ticks, then she went home with a comment that her behaviour had been good. If she had less than fifteen ticks, the sheet did not go home, and she was encouraged to try harder next time. Elizabeth was very keen on this idea and was quick to ask for her 'squared paper' (as she took to calling it) to be given to her on Mondays, and concerned if she missed any ticks. As she was not required to behave perfectly to win a tick, and as the weekly criterion for taking the sheet home was fairly low, she was successful in the main, and her behaviour was definitely better, in the teacher's opinion. However, discussion shortly afterwards with her mother showed that the system was breaking down at the home end. This discussion was held when, despite Elizabeth's assurances (not always to be trusted) that she had given her mother the sheet, the latter did not return it to school, signed, as she had promised to do. In addition, it seemed that mother had turned the reward strategy into a punishment one. Rather than praising Elizabeth for the ticks and positive comments, she had taken to remonstrating with her about blank boxes, and even more so about occasions when the sheet did not come home. Like many teachers, Elizabeth's mother found it very difficult to change her focus from bad behaviour to good behaviour. The teacher decided to abandon the reporting home aspect of the strategy. Elizabeth continued for some weeks with her squared paper, but her behaviour deteriorated somewhat. It was necessary to find another incentive.

The teacher had noticed how Elizabeth, as part of her general attention-seeking, loved the individual attention of adults. Visitors to the school, for instance, could be sure of her close attendance and sometimes found her quite appealing. It was decided, therefore, to change the nature of her not infrequent visits to the headteacher. Instead of being sent when she was in trouble, she was now sent as a reward for good behaviour. Her squared paper was kept as before. Each day when she had earned at least four ticks, she was allowed to go at the end of the day for ten minutes of the head's individual attention, to talk about anything she liked. The head took care that these discussions never turned into recriminations, whatever the circumstances. On Elizabeth's bad days, she was not seen by the head, unless some extreme misbehaviour had taken place. The head took care that any such meetings were held at a different time. End-of-the-day meetings with Elizabeth were always to be pleasant.

The strategy worked well. Elizabeth's behaviour remained far from perfect, of course, but at least she was able to remain in the school, despite the early fears of the staff that she would end up by being excluded. As her behaviour improved, her teacher was progressively more able to feel sympathetic about her difficulties, and the other pupils were less antagonistic towards her.

This case study illustrates how, even when a child is fairly clearly disturbed, it is often profitable to address the associated classroom behaviour directly, as Elizabeth's misbehaviour was clearly disrupting the work and learning of both herself and the other pupils. It could not, in their interests, be allowed to go on while long-term family therapy, or whatever psychological treatment was deemed appropriate, took its course. The key to the relative success of this classroom strategy lies in the trouble taken to find a reward that would be valued by Elizabeth, and to replace that (her mother's approval) with something equally desirable when her mother was not able to fulfil her undertaking. The benefits to Elizabeth of this strategy were probably considerable: not only was she able to behave well enough to remain in school, but her relatively improved relations with her peers, and her success in getting adult attention for good rather than bad behaviour would all help to improve her obviously poor self-concept.

An interesting postscript to this tale is that one day the teacher was informed by a spokesperson that the class had held a meeting, and decided to protest. They all wanted squared paper. The teacher, by explaining that Elizabeth needed the squared paper because she was having difficulties in settling into her new school, and that when she had settled as well as the others she would no longer need it, managed to quell the uprising. However, this incident illustrates neatly the need for teachers to strive for fairness and consistency with regard to rules, rewards and punishments, and to justify to pupils any real or apparent deviation from these principles.

5. Survival

Most case studies in books like this (and in this one) tell of successes, either complete or pretty nearly so; here in the interests of truth and of creating realistic aspirations in the reader, I shall finish with a story of survival rather than success in somewhat difficult circumstances, illustrating why survival is sometimes the best that can be hoped for, given the tasks presented to teachers.

The class in question was a boys (42 in number) second-year, low-ability secondary class called 2E in a streamed comprehensive school. My task was to see them for one 40-minute period a week (my only contact with them) for what was an extra

'They all wanted squared paper.'

Religious Education period. The standard allocation was one period for this subject, but due to the difficulties of timetabling in a large school, this class needed a 'filler' of some sort and someone with either an evangelistic or humorous cast of mind had decided it should be an extra period of RE, to be taught by anyone who happened to be free at that time. This opportunity fell to me. It was further decided that the content of this extra course should be Biblical knowledge. This was at a time when knowledge of any sort was a somewhat suspect component of any syllabus and thus Biblical knowledge was thin on the ground in the standard RE course the boys were receiving. The extra period was seen as a chance to fill this cultural gap.

The control problems thus presented to me were many. A phrase commonly used by the staff to describe this class was 'barrel of monkeys' and when I first met them this seemed a not unfair description, if a little hard on the monkey species. As a group they did not in the main regard any of their work as very important and saw RE and especially extra RE as perhaps their lowest priority for serious endeavour. Their main aim in the classroom, as possibly in life itself, was to have a carry-on. Like the proverbial barrel of monkeys, however, they were mischievous and boisterous, rather than nasty.

In addition to these basic difficulties, I had some others. The school was overcrowded and teachers did not always have the luxury of their own classrooms; I met the class immediately after taking another one some distance away, and could not be in the room until a few minutes after the boys had arrived there. This meant that my first task was often to quell a mini-riot or intervene to stop a quarrel turning into a fight. Only then could I belatedly begin the lesson in a far from perfect atmosphere.

Also, the classroom was on the ground floor and had windows looking on to an enclosed area with flower beds along the window walls. This sounds very pleasant: the problem was that during the period I was taking 2E a class of third-year boys, in the course of a gardening lesson, had the job of tending these flower beds. This third-year class was not renowned for its studious approach to its work either, and its members enjoyed (when not under the direct gaze of their supervising teacher) making rude faces and occasionally gestures at members of my class who, of course, were strongly motivated to reciprocate in the interests of preserving their honour.

The work I had to carry out was straightforward enough and presented no great academic challenge to me or the boys. All I had to do was read them a Bible story (or other extract) from a collection of these in everyday language or on occasion from the Bible itself, and hold a follow-up discussion on the meaning of the story, what lessons people might learn from it, and so on.

As might be imagined, these lessons did not always go as smoothly as I would have liked. After the initial problem of getting them settled, the class generally listened reasonably well to the story, but found it very difficult to join in a whole-class discussion in a civilised way. Waiting politely for your turn in a group of forty is difficult for anyone, and when these boys had an idea, especially one they thought others might laugh at, they tended to shout it out. The subject matter, of course, contained a fair amount of potential for merriment, Samson and Delilah being a particular favourite, as I remember. These occasions of disruption, together with those caused by the grotesque faces occasionally presented at the window, led to rather a chaotic second half to the lesson. Reprimands from me, followed by the usual standard punishments, succeeded only in antagonising the class, initially pretty good-natured, but not in making them behave significantly better. Understandably, they seemed to have genuine difficulty in remaining calm in this kind of situation.

I considered what might improve things. Three strategies occurred to me, all to do with changing the 'stimulus situation', as a behaviourist would call it. The first was to arrange with senior staff that it would be acceptable to dismiss my previous class, luckily a senior one composed of solid citizens, a few minutes early, to enable me to be present in the room before 2E arrived. This had a very calming effect: on the first occasion I can remember the surprised and slightly disappointed looks on the faces of the boys as they arrived, ready for a caper, only to find me there before them.

The second strategy was, again before the boys arrived, to lower and close the Venetian blinds with which the room was fortunately equipped, and to stand at the window side of the room to forestall any move to raise them by pupils anxious for enlightenment of the literal sort as well as the religious. This required the classroom lights to be kept switched on, of course, to the disquiet of a janitor who had to be convinced that the cost in electricity was educationally justified. This tactic was totally successful in removing the distraction of the faces at the window and consequent misbehaviour.

The third tactic I tried was to break down the class into smaller groups for the discussion part of the lesson. My intention here was to remove some of the frustration the boys obviously felt in waiting for their say in such a large class, and to lessen the over-exciting effect of the reaction of such a large audience when someone gave an answer considered funny or risqué. This I abandoned, however. The boys were unused to small group discussion and many tended to act the clown rather than under-take it seriously except when their group had the benefit of my direct supervision and participation. With six groups of about six this could not be for a large part of each group's time. Some movement of furniture was also required and resulted in ex-cuses for misbehaviour, such as bumping into one another, which, of course, were fully capitalised upon. We reverted to the format of reading followed by whole-class discussion.

The main remaining problem was thus the misbehaviour during the discussion. To tackle this, I explained again the nature of and need for civilised discussion. Without a good discussion, prop-erly listened to, I maintained, the boys could not really form an adequate understanding of the significance of the story. There-fore, if they made it impossible for me to hold such a discussion, I would abandon it and instead dictate a note to them about the story, an activity I correctly felt would be regarded as highly undesirable by many of them. The 'impossibility of continuing' I defined as a state of affairs which would be brought about by three inappropriate interruptions of any kind.

This produced a definite improvement in behaviour during the discussions. However the 'three strikes and you're out' rule tended to result in about ten minutes of note-taking, which, despite my solemn justification of it, I did not really want any more than the boys did. I therefore changed from this punish-ment strategy to a reward one. I explained to the boys that immediately after the reading of the story I would dictate a very short note which would take only a few minutes if they behaved well. Once this was completed, we could get on to the discussion. The three strikes rule would still apply, however, and we would revert to supplementary note-taking if necessary.

Thus the discussion, which they liked, served as a reward for good behaviour during the note-taking and led to this being a very quiet if short spell of time, creating a favourable atmosphere for starting the discussion. It was only necessary to revert (with an air of great disappointment, of course) to note-taking on a few occasions, just often enough for the boys to learn that I would carry out this threat if required.

A further aid to good order towards the ends of the lessons became available when I realised that the classroom being used was quite close to the school dining hall and that this was the period just before lunch. In this large school it was a highly prized achievement to be at the head of the long lunch queue, to get the food at its best, avoid waiting and be one up on rival classes. 2E were no exception to this rule and I therefore explained that I would be highly delighted to help them achieve this goal by having them lined up ready to leave on the bell, so long as they co-operated in finishing the lesson in good time and lined up in near silence and perfect order. This edible/social reward proved to be very powerful and led to the ends of the lessons becoming very peaceful indeed.

By using these strategies a fair degree of order was created out of chaos. As I have already stated, survival or a quiet life was my modest goal here. My reasons for settling for this were as follows. First, seeing things from the boys' point of view, it was unrealistic to expect them to take these lessons very seriously; they were not very keen on lessons in general, and certainly not on an extra RE period which they (and I) knew was a time-filler. Second, this was my only contact with the class each week; I did not feel that I had the time to create much in the way of a relationship with them, nor to do a great deal for their religious sensibilities or even knowledge. Third, to be frank, the work of this extra class was not one of my high priorities.

The strategies I used were a mixed bag. A good deal was achieved by changing aspects of the situation which were contributing to the misbehaviour. Getting to the room before your class is always desirable, as stated in an earlier chapter, but here it required the co-operation of senior staff (and my admission to them of a problem) to allow me to achieve this. Being able to use blinds to remove the faces at the window was a tactic not always likely to be available, but failing this an appeal to the teacher in charge of the faces and co-operation with him in dealing with the problem might have helped.

Turning to rewards and punishments, it must be admitted that using note-taking as a punishment for misbehaviour during discussion, however successful, is not really educationally desirable when one hopes to have pupils regard it as a useful study skill. For this reason alone it was more satisfactory to make discussion a reward for good behaviour during note-taking; this was also of course a more positive strategy, more likely to lead to the boys seeing me as being 'on their side', i.e. wanting them to succeed in moving on to a more desired activity. The 'early feeding' reward also helped in making the boys more positive to me, although they knew of course that I was using this to obtain a peaceful end to the lesson.

I survived.

◆ ◆ ◆

The case studies presented in this chapter illustrate, I believe, how the basic behavioural techniques of reward and punishment can be profitably employed in the classroom in a reflective way. Such reflection should involve consideration of the need to build a warm, positive relationship between teacher and pupils and the likely effects of particular rewards and punishments upon this relationship. In addition, thought must be given by the teacher to how the pupils themselves might see their behaviour, the situations in which it occurs and the ways in which the teacher attempts to influence it.

Useful principles illustrated in this chapter

Case 1

- An activity whose purpose is primarily to facilitate control may seem to waste teaching time, but may actually cost less time than the misbehaviour it prevents.

- Work easy enough to be carried out successfully by pupils with low attainment can significantly improve their academic self-esteem.

Case 2

- A control strategy which pupils find fun can improve teacher–pupil relationships as well as behaviour.

- Often annoying misbehaviour is not intentional, but is the result of previous learning and/or over-enthusiasm.

Case 3

- With a generally badly behaved class, it is better to try calmly to accept their existing ways of behaving as a necessary starting-point from which to bring about change than to feel angry or upset by it.

- Peer group approval rather than teacher praise is more likely to be effective as a reward with a class which seems indifferent to the teacher and her views.

- When a group token reward system is set up, it is important that some groups do not fall far behind the others; to the extent that this happens, an occasional special reward helps to obviate the adverse effects.

Case 4

- Even when a pupil seems clearly disturbed and in need of specialised psychological help, it is sometimes necessary and profitable to address classroom misbehaviour in a direct way.

- When a pupil's misbehaviour is frequent and general, it can be more practicable to direct a reward strategy at obtaining reasonable behaviour over set periods of time rather than try to target a large number of types of misbehaviour.

- It is important not to let a strategy of rewarding a certain desired behaviour turn into one of punishing the failure to produce that behaviour.

Case 5

- In difficult circumstances teachers may have to settle for survival rather than success.

- A good deal of misbehaviour can be prevented by changing the stimulus situations that provoke or facilitate it.

- While a less desired activity can act as a punishment for misbehaviour during a more desired one, it can be more effective to reverse the order of activities and use the more desired one as a reward for good behaviour during the less desired one.

Discussion questions

For each of the case studies

1. Identify the behavioural and cognitive elements of the approach taken. To what extent do you think these are compatible?

2. How effective, in your view, was the approach taken? Can you think of a different approach that might have given better results? Have you come across a problem like this in school? How did you or the teacher or the school deal with it?

7

PERENNIAL
PROBLEMS

Every class, every teacher and every control difficulty is unique. However, whenever teachers or student-teachers begin to discuss their experiences of pupil misbehaviour, smiles and frowns of recognition appear as they realise that many of their most worrying control problems have been encountered by others in very similar form. In this final chapter, I intend to identify some of the most common of such problems and to try to provide solutions for them or at least some helpful advice on them from a BRR perspective.

The source of these problems has been the simple procedure of asking successive classes of students to raise their most worrying 'What do you do about . . .?' questions at the end of courses on control, to be answered by myself and, on occasion, a visiting experienced teacher. Pooling the results of offering this opportunity to a fairly large number of groups produces a list of twelve of the most frequently raised questions—a discipline 'dirty dozen'.

Before I go on to list and attempt to answer them, a number of points need to be made. First, they come from students, and are therefore the kinds of difficulty which may be typical of a teacher and class in their early stages together rather than when a positive working relationship has been developed. So the last R of BRR will figure less prominently in my answers than it might for a set produced by more experienced teachers. Second, although it would sometimes be reasonable to say that if a teacher had taken the kind of approach outlined in the previous chapters she would be unlikely to find herself facing a particular problem, I shall still try to offer a solution. Third, I am not claiming that these are the twelve most common or difficult problems teachers experience, merely that they were common ones for the student-teachers I asked. In attempting to provide advice on them I am hoping not just to offer help with these particular difficulties, but to exemplify the ways of dealing with control problems that stem from the approach to discipline outlined in the previous chapters. Fourth, in these answers I shall not hesitate to give my personal views in a forthright way without constantly using phrases like 'in my opinion'. Fifth, this list of problems was compiled before I started writing, and is certainly not a set of problems carefully chosen to allow the easy application of the approach outlined in the previous chapters. Lastly, as stated earlier, action taken to deal with these or any other problems must always be in line with school policy. Here is the list (not in order of popularity).

What do you do about . . .?

(1) Pupils always asking out to the toilet.
(2) A generally too-high noise level.
(3) Being unable to identify the perpetrator of an offence when all deny guilt.
(4) A playground dispute which continues in the classroom.
(5) A pupil who simply refuses to do what he's told.
(6) Swearing in the classroom.
(7) Over-familiarity.
(8) Pupils who hit others.
(9) A class which enters the room or area in an over-excited way and is difficult to settle.
(10) Pupils who run about wildly out of their seats.
(11) Persistent disruption of a lesson by a pupil or pupils.
(12) A physical fight in the classroom.

In discussing these problems, I shall first reflect upon them, trying to see the situations from the pupils' points of view and to understand why they are behaving like this. A teacher who has got to know her pupils and built up a sound relationship with them will be in a good position to decide just which of the possible motives for each type of misbehaviour applies in any particular instance of it. In what follows, not knowing the pupils involved, I shall focus on what seem to me to be the most likely motives. Having thus reflected on the causes of the behaviour, I shall go on to suggest what might be done to change it or otherwise cope with it.

As stated above, in these analyses the relationship aspect of the BRR approach cannot be given as much weight as it would normally merit. In general, though, I believe that with the kind of teacher–pupil relationship described earlier as desirable, problems like these are less likely to occur, and if they do, the suggestions offered below are more likely to work.

1. Pupils always asking out to the toilet

This problem seems to present itself at both primary and secondary stages and causes a great deal of concern to beginning teachers. There are various reasons for these repeated requests, such as forgetting to go at break time; wanting a break from the classroom (especially if the teacher will let two chums go together); wanting out of the classroom in order to get up to some mischief; being reluctant to go at break because of others' unruly behaviour in the toilets. There is also the possibility of a pupil having a physical health problem.

This is an area where there should be a clear school policy, but in many schools much is left to the judgment of the individual teacher. There are obvious age factors: in many primary schools the youngest pupils are allowed to go on request, perhaps being reminded of the need to go at break. With older primary and secondary pupils, it is usual to expect them to go only at break.

If the last reason given above (a physical problem) ever seems to be the case, and this has not been brought to your attention by the appropriate senior colleague, you should err on the side of caution and let the pupil go, but inform the senior colleague as soon as possible, so that the matter can be looked into. If you have reason to believe that pupils are reluctant to use the toilets at break because of unruly behaviour you should also bring this to the attention of your seniors. For healthy older primary and secondary pupils it is obviously desirable to minimise time away from work, including trips to the toilet.

General strategies that can be employed include (for younger children) frequent reminders to go at break, checking after break that they have gone and praising or otherwise rewarding them; letting only one go at a time; requiring all pupils leaving the room for any reason to write their names on a list by the door, scoring them out on return (this also provides a record of how often pupils go out, and is very useful at a fire-drill or indeed fire). A particular concern of many inexperienced teachers is how to decide whether a request is genuine or not. Without knowing the pupil well, it is very difficult to tell: a strategy which seems to work, however, is to ask the pupil quietly whether he is able to last out till break, and, if he says he isn't, to tell him to ask again in a minute or two. Generally, only the genuine seem to ask again.

2. A generally too-high noise level

Most students who mention this as a main problem stress that they do not see it as involving deliberate misbehaviour by pupils, except insofar as it tends to be associated with a reluctance to settle to steady work. I believe that this difficulty stems initially from the teacher's failure to make it clear that a low level of working noise is appropriate in class and to take steps to establish this as a norm. There are various other contributory causes. There is a 'vicious spiral' effect—as the noise rises, pupils must talk more and more loudly to be heard; if pupils are unsure what to do or how to do it there is an increased need to talk to others; if they are afraid of doing the wrong thing they will tend to ask others; if they need to move about a good deal to get materials their movements and incidental chat to others will make noise; and, of course, all of us at times prefer pleasant chat to work, and in a generally noisy class-room it is difficult to concentrate on work.

To establish the right level of working noise (which will differ, of course, for different teachers) what you must first try to do is to organise your classroom so as to minimise the need and the excuse for chat and movement. Clear instructions, work at an appropriate level of difficulty, well-organised resources, etc. (see chapter 3) will all help. Then explain the need for a quiet at-mosphere, in terms, of course, of the benefits it brings to the pupils. Set them to work, stopping and quietening them when the noise level has risen as far as you are willing to accept. After a very short period of silent work allow the noise to rise again, and so on. If the pupils are genuinely not really wanting to misbehave, they will soon learn the new norm. Playing a game, 'How long can you work in total silence?' (starting with a min-ute as the target) is good fun, helps to keep your relationship a pleasant one and creates some welcome peace and quiet. Watch out for the opportunity to reward groups or individuals for working quietly and have times when steam can be legitimately let off, such as playing games.

3. Being unable to identify the perpetrator of an offence when all deny guilt

Beginning teachers often report this difficulty. Without knowing exactly who has committed an offence, such as causing a loud disruptive noise, they make an issue of it, demanding to know who has done it, often in an angry way, to be met by a chorus of denials. The teacher has thus compounded her problem. As well as the disruption, she now has another offence to deal with: someone is telling a lie. Why do pupils behave like this? There are various possible reasons: for example, fear of the con-sequences of confession; once having denied guilt, reluctance to admit to a lie by later admission; a feeling of innocence stemming from not having meant to commit the offence, or from someone else also being responsible in part; a reluctance to lose face by confessing in such public circumstances; and, of course, a wish to annoy or defy the teacher.

This is a case where it would have been much better not to have got yourself into this position in the first place. If you had observed the situation in which the offence took place for just a little longer before asking who was guilty, you might have been able to identify the culprit from his own or others' behaviour; you certainly would have reacted in a calmer way. However, let us assume that you have asked the question and received the denials and that you have little idea who is guilty. If you have remained cool, you might be able to settle for a joke about a poltergeist or ventriloquist. If not, you may get a confession by saying that you will not be making a big deal of the matter if you find out who is guilty (thus rewarding good behaviour). This should reduce fear of punishment, as should saying that you know that others share the blame and, of course, doing your best not to be or seem angry.

More deviously (if you are prepared to be a little unethical) you might try asking the main suspect, 'Who made you do that?', or some other question that assumes his guilt but offers him a way out. A tactic to be avoided is punishing a whole group. This will cause resentment from the others and may lead to further undesired behaviour. If the gravity of the offence or your own desire not to lose face leads you into doing this, try to restrict it to occasions when you are pretty sure that all in the group know who is guilty and are therefore themselves guilty of something by not informing you, and tell them this. Overall, however, this is a situation much better to avoid than to have to deal with.

4. A playground dispute which continues in the classroom

Frequently teachers become irritated by pupils bringing their seemingly petty disputes from their free time or even from their time at home into the classroom, causing disruption to work through squabbles, arguments, huffs and even physical confrontations. Why do they do this? The simplest explanation is that the teacher has not clearly enough established in the minds of the pupils that the classroom is territory where different norms to those of the playground apply. This means that even in the classroom they continue to focus their attention on their current 'real-life' concerns, in this case their long-term feud or short-term squabble. Another possibility, especially with younger children, is that a pupil who brings a dispute into the classroom is trying to get the teacher to intervene to right some real or imagined wrong.

The initial problem you face in dealing with the situation is to decide how far to get involved. As a general principle, it is probably best to keep out of playground disputes, unless they seem to be serious, such as persistent bullying, about which many schools now have policies. If the problem is of this kind, you should inform senior staff about it, as there are clearly limits to a class teacher's authority outside her own classroom, and you don't want to bite off more than you can chew. If the problem is less serious, but is disruptive to the work of the class in that, say, certain pupils are refusing to co-operate with one another, then you may have to become involved.

First, try to make it clear that the classroom is different from the playground and that different behaviour is expected. More specifically, avoiding taking sides or believing one pupil's version of events rather than another's when you have no direct knowledge of what has happened. Rather, act as a referee between opponents, trying to get them to discuss their dispute reasonably and resolve it. You may find it useful to use the dispute as an opportunity for class discussion about fair play, sensible behaviour, etc. In such a discussion, you can try to guide pupils towards being generally more considerate to one another, and to see, for example, the unfairness of excluding one pupil from games. All of this should cool tempers and the attention being received should soothe the hurt feelings of pupils who feel ill-used.

However, be reasonable in your expectations of what you can achieve. A certain degree of nastiness in children's behaviour and attitudes towards one another is inevitable, and every child has to learn to cope with this without always calling upon adults to make others be nicer to them. Playground disputes provide such learning experiences, and, as stated above, you should in general try to avoid being drawn into them.

5. A pupil who simply refuses to do what he is told

A pupil who behaves in this way will usually know that his behaviour is serious in that it is a refusal to accept the teacher's and therefore the school's authority. Such behaviour may be calm defiance, or it may be that the pupil who does this is extremely angry, upset or even frightened.

The calmly defiant pupil is probably testing you out to see if you have the nerve to insist on remaining in charge of the classroom. If you are defied in this way, ask the pupil in as quiet, polite and confident a way as you can manage to do something which you are sure is within his capabilities, such as moving his position or carrying out a simple copying task. (If the refusal was to carry out some other task, leave this aside for the time being.) If he still refuses, say that you are going to give him some time to think about his refusal and its consequences, which you should explain in detail as being very serious indeed, ultimately involving the attention of the headteacher, as he is refusing to accept the authority of the school.

After a time, perhaps about ten minutes, in as quiet and non-public a way as possible (to lessen the loss of face for him) ask him again to undertake the simple task. This cooling-off period will often do the trick, so long as the pupil believes that you will carry out your threat to involve senior staff, as he will know that it will be much less trouble for him to do as you tell him. If he continues to defy you, you may give him a little more time to 'come to his senses', but after that you must, of course, show that you have meant what you have said and involve senior staff. If he refuses to go to the appropriate person you must be prepared to send a message to ask that person to come to the classroom. It is ironic that it is usually only if you are not sure that you will have the nerve to call upon senior staff that this might actually have to be done.

If a pupil who refuses to do what you tell him is very upset or angry, you should try to find out what has caused this and deal with it. Perhaps he feels he has been unfairly treated, or he is afraid of failing with a task in a humiliating way. After doing your best to put such things right and calm the pupil down, a quiet request to do something straightforward will often lead to compliance. If necessary, of course, the above procedure for coping with deliberate defiance can be gone through, but is unlikely to be needed.

Some teachers would add to this the advice that ultimately both kinds of refusing pupil should be made to obey the originally defied instruction, but I would settle for compliance with the second-stage one, unless compliance with the first is necessary for purposes other than control. If the pupil falls into line with the second, he has accepted your authority. As with all of the problems so far considered, a warm relationship between teacher and pupils will make this difficulty much less likely to occur and much easier to deal with if it does.

6. Swearing in the classroom

Swearing (by pupils) in class stems usually from one of three origins. It may be the result of inadequate learning (young children especially may not have learned that certain words are taboo in certain situations); it may be occasioned by a loss of temper or a startling experience; or it may be a deliberate attempt to shock or embarrass the teacher.

'. . . (Swearing) may be occasioned by a loss of temper or a startling experience.'

The single most important point here is never to appear shocked or to moralise, making out that decent people never swear, etc. Your pupils know as well as you do that this is simply not the case, and you don't want them to think that you can so easily be upset. The message to try to get across is that swearing is inappropriate in the classroom, which is a place for polite, businesslike behaviour. If the swearing has been caused by a pupil being startled, or simply not realising that a word is rude, correct the pupil in a quiet way, but do not punish or appear annoyed. Teach young children that such words are rude and not suitable in class (it is a good idea to suggest milder expletives, more suited to the classroom) and try to find opportunities to praise or other-wise reward more acceptable vocabulary when it occurs.

When swearing seems to be a deliberate attempt to shock, em-barrass or defy you, the best approach is to treat this like any other piece of insolence, without making much of the swearing, except that it makes the offence more serious. It is particularly important not to give any sign of being shocked, upset or an-gered in this case.

7. Over-familiarity

Most teachers like to be friendly and relaxed with their pupils, a desire with which I entirely sympathise. However, some find that this kind of relationship can lead to pupils being over-familiar, in the sense of sometimes treating the teacher as being just one of the gang, a friendly adult with no more power than anyone else in the classroom. As well as being rather embarrass-ing when, say, colleagues are present, such an attitude makes it difficult when the teacher needs, for example, to direct pupils to get on with their work, instead of having a chat.

If you find yourself in this position, either you have inherited the problem from a previous teacher, or, more likely, it has resulted from one of two possible errors. The first of these possibilities is that you have tried to be democratic in too literal a way. It is a good idea to be democratic in the restricted sense of, say, dis-cussing a rule with pupils and letting them express their views before you finally formulate the rule, but it is misguided to give pupils the idea that they have an equal say to yours. They do not. It is your responsibility to be in charge of the class; if, for example, someone is hurt because of unruly behaviour, you will normally be held responsible. Along with this responsibility must go power.

The second possibility is that in an attempt to get difficult pupils to co-operate you have been too friendly with them, believing that if they are your friends they will be nice to you and do what you ask them. Such attempts by teachers to ingratiate themselves with pupils are usually disastrous. Rather than making pupils friendly and co-operative, they are likely to lead to them holding the teacher in contempt.

This is another situation it is much better never to get into (and if you follow the advice given in previous chapters you will not get into it), but, assuming that your pupils are being over-familiar, what should you do? Make it clear to pupils, without showing annoyance, exactly how you wish to be approached and addressed (the 'hands up' rule for all group situations is a must if you have this problem). Make it clear, also, that when you give an instruction it must be followed. If pupils approach you in the old way, simply ignore them with a puzzled expression. If this doesn't produce the required behaviour, correct them and reprimand them (if necessary) in a quiet way. Avoid showing any sign of anger or upset. Be totally consistent in requiring the new behaviour. If you occasionally accept the old behaviour you are engaging in intermittent reinforcement, which is the best way to keep it going. Make a point of noticing and commending appropriate behaviour, especially from previously over-familiar pupils. Take great care that you are not being over-familiar towards the pupils. If you are cheeky or rude to them as a joke you are inviting the same sort of behaviour in return, and you cannot reasonably object to it.

8. Pupils who hit others

Teachers find that there are some pupils who frequently hit others, causing much consequent disruption, such as attempts by victims to hit back and the need for the teacher to deal with hurt feelings and bodies and demands for retribution. Why do pupils behave like this? This way of reacting to real or imagined slights from other pupils often indicates that the pupil involved comes from a home environment where this is a normal way of behaving with family and friends. Pupils like this may well have

'Deal firmly and dismissively with any "He hit me first" excuses.'

been told to stand up for themselves in this physical way, for example to hit back harder whenever they feel they have been pushed or shoved. Such hitting is therefore best seen as a learned habit, capable of change, though resistant to it. Hitting is also, of course, a way to assert oneself, if one finds it difficult to do so in more acceptable ways, and to attain power over others. And, sadly, some pupils will get pleasure from inflicting pain upon others and causing fear.

Teachers should not allow hitting of any sort, however slight, for whatever reason. An absolute ban on physical violence is the best rule. Treat any incidence as serious. Demand instant cessation, reprimand, explain how serious the offence is. Deal firmly and dismissively with any 'He hit me first' excuses. (Although, of course, you will have to investigate such allegations, being hit first cannot be allowed to excuse hitting in a non-violent classroom.) Make it clear that any hitting is wrong and explain why. In a class where this is a recurring problem, make sure that you take opportunities to praise or otherwise reward non-violent ways of dealing with problems, especially if used by a pupil given to hitting. Try to get pupils to accept that they should bring significant grievances to the teacher, rather than take the law into their own hands. This means, of course, that you have to be prepared to spend some time on sorting out disputes. Useful short-term tactics are to keep hitter and current victim as physically far apart as possible in the classroom, and to stagger their departure from class by detaining one for a few moments.

9. A class which enters the room or area in an over-excited way and is difficult to settle

An extreme case of this was dealt with in one of the case studies in chapter 6, so a brief treatment will suffice here. As stated then, this problem usually arises from the immediate previous experience of the class, such as capering or otherwise getting over-excited in the playground or corridor, or previous class in a secondary school. If in addition the pupils have been entering your room and getting away with such behaviour for a while, this will have acted as a reward for it, with the usual consequences.

It would normally be highly effective in changing this behaviour to change the stimulus which has occasioned it. This will probably not often be possible, as you will not usually have much control over what happens before you receive the class. This is one reason, in passing, why it is a good idea for teachers to agree to undertake corridor duties in a school. If corridors are peaceful, there is a better chance that classrooms will also be peaceful. Try to be at the door of the room as the pupils arrive, slowing down the flow and marking the change of territory and norms. Have work ready to do whenever possible (ideally already set out on desks), well within pupils' capabilities, so that there is less excuse not to settle. 'Straight to seats' and 'Hands up if you want anything' are rules which will help with this problem, as they will with many others. Point out and reward appropriate settling down by individuals or groups. And try not to get angry with the class, as this is a very bad start to your lesson. Remember that this misbehaviour is not directed at you. It is probably the result of what has happened earlier, before you were in charge of the class.

10. Pupils who run about wildly out of their seats

Again, I believe that if you had followed the advice given in earlier chapters, you would not be in the position of having to deal with this problem. However, given that you are, what should you do? Why has this state of affairs developed? If a class often behaves like this the most likely cause is that some pupils have behaved in this way out of high spirits, or in continuation of some playground dispute or game, got away with it, and found it and the teacher's inadequate response enjoyable and therefore rewarding. It has therefore become an established habit, with other pupils joining in the fun.

The answer to this one, of course, is to establish incompatible behaviour, that is a norm that pupils stay in their places unless there is a legitimate reason for leaving them. As far as possible, set work that requires little movement. Take every opportunity to reward appropriate movement about the room, watch out for unnecessary movement or running, stop the child involved and make him go back and retrace his steps (if legitimate) in an appropriate manner. It may be necessary for a while to require pupils to ask permission to leave their seats, at least during some kinds of work. If you can keep an eagle eye on the class and manage to stop the first offender of this kind on each occasion, you will have solved the problem. As usual, avoid becoming angry or flustered, as this will act as a reward to those pupils who enjoy upsetting the teacher.

If you suddenly find yourself in the position of having to calm a class which is running about wildly, a good tactic, as mentioned in an earlier chapter, is firstly to get the attention of the class by making a loud noise (a bang is better than shouting), then to focus attention on one pupil by bringing him to a suitable place in the room and addressing him. The others will normally quieten down to find out what is going to happen, and you will thus have calmed the riot.

11. Persistent disruption of a lesson by a pupil or pupils

This is one of the kinds of misbehaviour teachers dislike most, firstly because it is very difficult not to take it personally and secondly because it spoils a lesson that has taken a lot of time and trouble to prepare. There are two main probable causes of such behaviour: attention-seeking and the deliberate desire to challenge the teacher's authority and to try to get her to lose her equanimity.

If you feel that attention-seeking is the cause, interruptions can be ignored up to a point, if they are not too extreme or persistent. However, it is very difficult not to show reinforcing signs of annoyance. It will therefore often be necessary, after a calm warning or two (but not too many) to move the offender to a place out of sight of the others with a straightforward individual task to do, assuring him that when he shows he has learned to behave sensibly he will be allowed to rejoin the class. Deliberate disruption is a more serious problem. It is even more important to remain calm here, for often a large part of the motivation for a pupil behaving like this is to upset you. The strategy just outlined for the mere attention-seeker should be tried. If the pupil continues to disrupt even after being moved, he should be warned about the seriousness of his offence. He is preventing the main purpose of the school, that is that pupils should learn, from being achieved, and he will have to bear the consequences of this. Be prepared to abandon the lesson, apologising to the other pupils. Make sure that what follows in its place is something less attractive, but don't fall into the trap of punishing or blaming the whole class: this will be unfair to at least some and will antagonise them. Offer to try to hold the lesson later (and do so). Try to be relaxed about this, but, without nagging, get across the message that it is the pupils who may lose the lesson, not you. If disruption still continues after all this, you should not hesitate to involve senior staff, for the point made above is true: this pupil is stopping others from learning, which is the main purpose of the school.

12. A physical fight in the classroom

This is a rare event in most schools, but it can be very alarming, especially for a beginning teacher, which is probably why it appears in this set of problems. Usually the cause is a squabble between pupils, sometimes continued from the playground, sometimes part of an ongoing feud. One loses his temper and hits out, the other retaliates and you have a fight on your hands.

A fight in the classroom, unlike playground fights, is unlikely to be a premeditated event and will very often peter out quickly, as the protagonists realise where they are. If it does not you must, of course, try to stop it. Avoid physical contact if at all possible, as it entails the dangers of your being hurt, getting angry, losing authority if you fail to stop the fight and even being accused of assaulting the fighters. Loudly instruct the pupils to stop. This will create a pause and give them the chance to end the fight, which they might well welcome. At a moment when no fists are flying, place yourself between the opponents. They are extremely unlikely to attack you in order to come to blows again. Tell them to sit down and calmly ask why they are fighting, in order to start them talking, which is incompatible with continuing the fight. (If these steps do not work, this is an occasion when you should send a pupil for a senior member of staff.)

Once they have stopped, it is highly unlikely they will start again, at least in the classroom. Punishment from you is probably unnecessary, as the pupils have not deliberately misbehaved. However, you must inform senior staff about the fight, so that they will be able to take action about such a serious matter, for instance take steps to prevent a return match after school, investigate the cause of the trouble and prepare themselves for possible parental visits.

♦ ♦ ♦

So much for the dirty dozen. I hope that my views on how to cope with these problems will help you to decide how you will tackle them if and when you encounter them, and also that I have succeeded in illustrating the general approach to control that I have outlined in the previous chapters.

Useful principles illustrated in this chapter

- There can be many different reasons for difficult behaviour such as repeated requests to go to the toilet.

- If keeping a class generally quiet is a problem, it can help to have some legitimately noisy times.

- It is not usually productive to punish a whole class or group for the actions of one or two pupils, as this will create resentment.

- Avoid taking sides in a dispute unless you can be sure that one pupil is clearly in the wrong.

- Give a defiant pupil time to cool off and think about the consequences for him of his defiance if continued.

- Avoid appearing shocked or upset by inappropriate behaviour like swearing.

- Do not allow pupils to form the impression that they have an equal say to yours in the classroom.

- Do not accept any physical violence whatsoever in the classroom.

- Being at the entrance to the classroom or area as pupils arrive facilitates control and signals a change of territory and norms.

- To get the attention of a whole noisy class, focus attention on one pupil after a loud signal.

- If a lesson or activity has to be abandoned because of disruption, make it clear the loss is the pupils', not the teacher's.

- Avoid physical contact with pupils if trying to stop them fighting.

Discussion questions

For each of the problems:

1. Do you think the guidelines offered in this chapter are likely to be helpful for coping with this difficulty? What changes would you suggest?

2. Have you ever experienced this problem, or seen a teacher encounter it? If so, how did you/she try to deal with it, and how successful was this?

A LAST WORD

In a book like this it is inevitable that I should have concentrated on some of the difficulties of teaching. As you probably already well know, it is a job that also has many pleasures. I believe that if you try to achieve control of the kind and in the ways I have described, taking **reflective** account of your pupils' **behaviour** and your **relationships** with them, you will have taken a very important step towards creating an atmosphere in which you and they can experience these pleasures. Good luck with your efforts.

SOME SUGGESTED
FURTHER READING

Clarizio, H.F. (1980) *Toward Positive Classroom Discipline* (Third edition). New York: John Wiley & Sons.

Docking, J.W. (1980) *Control and Discipline in Schools: Perspectives and Approaches.* London: Harper & Row.

Fontana, D. (1985) *Classroom Control: Understanding and Guiding Classroom Behaviour.* London and New York: The British Psychological Society and Methuen.

Johnstone, M., and Munn, P. (1987) *Discipline in School: A Review of 'Causes' and 'Cures'.* Edinburgh: The Scottish Council for Research in Education.

Montgomery, D. (1989) *Managing Behaviour Problems.* Sevenoaks, Kent: Hodder & Stoughton.

Wheldall, K., and Glynn, T. (1989) *Effective Classroom Learning: a Behavioural Interactionist Approach to Teaching.* Oxford and New York: Basil Blackwell.

The Elton Report (1989) (*Discipline in Schools: Report of The Committee of Enquiry chaired by Lord Elton.*) London: HMSO.

INDEX

Accountability, 43–8
Answering in turns, 47
Approval, 73, 77
   peer, 73, 90, 103, 110
   social, 80, 109
   teacher, 79, 103
Attainment, 24
Attention, focusing, 48, 138
Attention seeking, 55, 79
Attitudes, 15, 19, 20

Baseline, 56, 62
Behaviour, *throughout*
Behavioural, reflective,
    relationship (BRR) approach,
    ix, 53–65, 64
   in action, 97–121
   ethical criticisms of, 91–2
   practical criticisms of, 92–3
   principles of, 64–5
   putting it into practice, 69–93
Behavioural approach, 54–6
Behaviourist psychology, 53
Being thoughtful and analytical,
   28
Believing in the value of learning,
   23–4
Blaming whole class, 48
Break, 35, 50, 55
Bribery, 90–1
Bullying, 129

Calmness, 25–6
Case studies, 97

Certificates, 24
'Change the system', 8
Class control, *throughout*
Class in chaos, 48
Classroom
   atmosphere, 102, 105
   climate, 33
   furniture, 37, 118
Cognitive approach, 56–60
Cognitive psychology, 53
Competition, 74, 101
Confidence, 27
Consistency, 49, 114
Cooling-off period, 130
Copying, 38
Corporal punishment, 92
Counselling, 7

Defiance, 59, 130–1
Demeanour, 15, 19, 20
Detachment, 26–7, 62
Detention, 84, 87, 107
Determination, 24–5
Disadvantage, 9
Disapproval, peer, 79, 103
Disruption, 61
   deliberate, 138
   persistent, 138
Disturbance, 113
   psychological, 4, 6
Disturbed children, 75

Exclusion, temporary, 87
Extinction, 54, 55, 89, 90–1

Extra-curricular activities, 22

Failure, 59
Fairness, 49, 114
Fallacies
  'interest', 4, 9–14
  psychological, 4–7
  sociological, 4, 8–9
  staffroom cynic's, 4, 14–15
Fighting, 139
Free time, 73, 75, 103

Games, 23, 73
Group co-operation, 74
Group friendship, 108
Group responses, 47
Group work, 34
Guilt, 1, 10, 82

Hand raising, 47
Health, 29
Hitting, 134–6
Homework, 22

Identifying perpetrator, 127–8
Incentive, 80, 86, 109
Incompatible activities, 40
Incompatible behaviour, 137
Independent work, 37
Individual responses, 47
Individual tasks, 82
Individual work, 34
Interpersonal strategies, 33, 43,
  43–50

Lightheartedness, 23
Logical consequences, 87

Making work interesting, 10, 57
Marking, 45
Misbehaviour, *throughout*
Mischievousness, 5, 23
Modelling, 89–90
Monitoring

behaviour, 45
behaviour across school, 88
work, 45
Motivation, intrinsic, 76

Nagging, 49, 84, 109, 139
Noise
  level, 126–7
  and movement, 43
Noisy and quiet activities, 40
Norms, 42, 99, 127, 129, 136, 137

Obedience, 19
Observational tasks, 28
Openness, 28–9
Open-plan school, 106
Organisation, 28
Organisational strategies, 33–43,
  43
Organising work, 34–5
Over-familiarity, 50, 133–4

Perennial problems, 124–140
Permissive approach, 7
Persistence, 24
Personal qualities, 19–30
Personality, 14, 15, 19, 20
Planning, 28
Playground dispute continuing
  in classroom, 128–30
Preferred activities, 73
Preventative strategies, 33
Protest against society, 9
Punctuality, 49
Punishment, 54, 55, 63, 69, 70, 82,
  120
  corporal, 82, 85
  delayed, 84
  ethical objections to, 83
  exercises, 87
  practical objections to, 83
  range of, 87
  trivial, 84
  use of, 82–9

of whole class, 138
of whole group, 128
Pupils
feelings of, 56, 64
getting to know, 43–5
leaving seats by, 104
leaving unattended, 46
liking, 21
motives of, 56, 64, 79
names of, 43
point of view of, 44, 78
thoughts of, 56, 64

Queues, 35
Quiz, 23

Records, 45
Recreational pursuits, 29
Reinforcement, 80
intermittent, 134
negative, 55
overkill, 75
Reinforcer, 54, 55
Relationships, 21, 22, 60, 61–2, 64,
87, 104, 105
Reprimands, 87
Resources, 27, 34
home-made, 37
organising, 36
Retribution, 23, 82, 86
Reward, 54, 55, 63, 69, 70, 80, 120
ethical objections to, 83
frequency of, 77
inappropriate use of, 81–2
intrinsic, 72, 76, 77, 91
levels of, 70, 75–7, 76
and punishment in
combination, 104, 106
ratio of to punishment, 78
tangible, 75
token, 73–5
use of, 71–82
whole class system, 109
Role, teacher's, 61

Rules, 8, 27, 70, 91, 104, 108
establishing, 40–3
Running in the classroom, 41, 137

Safety, 41, 43
Scheduling, 77
School policy, 41, 70, 89, 125
Seating arrangements, 82
and group co-operative work,
38
and individual work, 38
and whole class lessons, 38
Seating plans, 39 (fig.)
Self-concept, 29, 57, 62, 80, 114
academic, 57, 59, 101
enhancing, 80–1
Self-esteem, 102
Senior staff, 41, 46, 70, 93, 98,
131
Sense of humour, 20, 23
Settling a difficult class, 97–103,
136–7
'Shadowing', 5
Shared interests, 22
Shouting
by pupils, 103
by teacher, 48
Signals, 48
Sin-bin, 88
Standards, 40
Stimulus situation, changing, 117,
136
Storage, 36
Stress reduction, 26
Success, 60, 72–3, 76, 79, 103
Swearing in class, 131–3

Tasks, long-term, 34
Territory, 42, 129, 136
Therapy, 7
family, 113
Thinking positively, 29–30
Threats, 49
Time-out facility, 88

Toilet, asking out to, 125–6
Transition points, 47

Undermining, 76
Uniform, 22

Value of learning, believing in
    the, 23–4
Violence, 135

Withdrawal of privileges, 87